FREE ICE CREAM

Not just Ice cream . . .

It's free everything for everyone

GANESH NATARAJAN

This Book Was First Published by Edisun Consulting Services in 2021.

This book has been published with all efforts taken to make the material error free. However, the publisher does not assume and hereby disclaims any liability to any part for any loss, damage, or disruption caused by errors or omissions, whether such errors or omissions result from negligence, accident, or any other cause.

This book is a work of fiction and, except in the case of historical facts, any resemblance to actual persons, living or dead, is purely coincidental.

© Ganesh Natarajan 2021

Typeset by Edisun Consulting Services

An Imprint of Edisun Consulting Services
1067, Officers Colony
Anna Nagar West Extension
Chennai – 600101
publishing@iamanauthor.in
www.indie-bookstore.com | www.iamanauthor.in

ABOUT THE AUTHOR

Ganesh Natarajan started his life in Neyveli, a small town in South India, with an industrial complex comprising a coal mine, a thermal power station and a fertilizer plant. On completing school, he started his career as a marine engineer, sailing around the world. In the mid-90s, he migrated to Australia, starting his land-based career, and continues to provide physical asset management consulting services to the industry.

Over his career, he has had exposure to varied industries including shipping, mining, utilities, petrochemicals and manufacturing industries such as metal, food and beverage, plastic, building products, pulp and paper manufacturing.

Ganesh currently lives in Melbourne with his wife and two daughters and takes an active interest in the spheres of emerging technology, global economics and politics.

FREE ICE CREAM

Not just ice cream . . .

It's free everything for everyone

GANESH NATARAJAN

CONTENTS

FOREWORD

BY PROF. R VAIDYANATHAN

April 2nd, 2021

For a person who for a lifetime (and a half) has been dabbling with engineering concepts, this is a refreshingly new area, economic idealism, as I call it.

I read a part of the manuscript a few months ago (the latter part was probably not written then). I didn't like it, to be frank. How can anything be free? I tried to pick holes in the basic idea, but could not.

Then I consoled myself saying solar power is for free. That generates wind power as well. For that matter, solar power grows trees and provides all forms of fossil fuels, indirectly. Solar power is the basic currency. If that is free, why not avail that and make every other thing free!

Mr Natarajan has not rested on the basic idea alone. He has used his imagination to ponder over all possible technical, humanitarian and political aspects. As George rightly puts it, "The concept is radical, to say the least", the concept that originated from Mad Morty of Belgrave High.

I will not be surprised if in 50 years, the free everything concept really catches up. This book is not for entertainment alone. It will definitely make the reader think.

Considering that the author was a marine engineer two decades ago, he has made a creditable switch over as a writer and has handled a revolutionary idea with aplomb. I am sure this man will be writing many more books in future.

Prof. R Vaidyanathan is an educator, with a PhD from the Indian Institute of Technology, Madras. He has taught engineering at various levels for the last forty-seven years and has been at the forefront of technical education as the Principal of various engineering colleges. He is also the author of thirty research papers and seven technical books.

FOREWORD

BY DEEPAK DHAYANITHY

April 10th, 2021

Ganesh Natarajan tells us the amazing story of five precocious teenagers, their high school project – *Free Ice Cream*, a couple of great teachers, a disdainful yet caring elder brother, the lessons they learn over time and how it all shapes their friendships. The story is inspiring and evokes nostalgia in equal measure. One doesn't necessarily have to be a foodie or have ice-cream cravings to enjoy this book. The story is really a hard look at "Free", its economic, logical, sociological, political, business and ethical dimensions. It is the story of the tenacity of five teenagers and of the love and wisdom that their caring teachers shower upon them. When you close the book, you will find yourself rooting for at least one of its protagonists.

It may be the leader who eventually seizes the moment to "go big", roll her sleeves up and gets to ensuring that big *Free Ice Cream* ideas do get implemented. It may be the patriotic native who finds it imperative to give it all back to her home while still figuring out the idea of "home". It may be the ecologically and socially minded youngster who faces the harsh realities of the "business" of doing good. It may be the globe-trotting consultant who sees the "big picture". It may well be the smart kid who climbs the professional ladder rapidly, gets to control valuable resources, appears to only care about the greenback and yet displays unflinching support when it is most needed.

Mortimer and Prof Iyer are great teachers who not only instruct, but inspire and remain the glue long after school and beyond state and national borders. Their deep caring for the intellectual growth of their students as well as their wellbeing is well disguised by them posing seemingly impossible challenges. In that regard, *Free Ice Cream* would make you remember the great teachers you have had. It may also haunt you with ideas that were discarded or abandoned.

Ganesh's book embodies a vast amount of expertise in the sciences, economics and carries the flavour of a well-travelled writer. Just as breezy and direct, his words reveal an understated caring for his characters and how they grow up. For young readers, *Free Ice Cream* offers a framework for logical thought, critical argumentation, teamwork and more. It anticipates the vast amount of exploration ahead of them which may have just begun with the challenging project that they are faced with right now!

When you finish the book, it would certainly make you call your friends and ask about their wellbeing.

Deepak Dhayanithy is Associate Professor of Strategic Management at IIM Kozhikode. He has been at IIM Kozhikode since 2011, offering and teaching elective courses to MBA and PhD students on sports, analytics, decision-making, poker and strategy. He has written a number of articles in newspapers and is the author of Strategy Huddle: Management Lessons from Sports *(published in February 2021).*

FOREWORD

BY DEREK SMITH

—————

April 13th, 2021

Five business students are given a seemingly impossible task in this engaging tale by Ganesh Natarajan. Step by step, Meg, Chen, Karan, Miya and Emma challenge their initial assumptions and conventional business thinking in their quest to find a way to produce, of all things, free ice cream. Testing limits, using their youthful optimism and ingenuity, and gaining occasional but timely wisdom from a couple of respected elders, they manage to overcome their doubts and accomplish their mission – at least in theory.

Along the way, they learn valuable lessons about respecting each other's opinions, acknowledging their own weaknesses and how to work together as a genuine team. And they reach a startling conclusion – applying their new principles, they realise that it is possible to make not just free ice cream but free everything – for everybody!

Ganesh allows us to follow the journey of these five diverse characters using crisp dialogue, compelling plot development, logical argument and a sound basis of technological, political and economic reality.

So, is it really possible to provide everything free for everybody? Read this. And ask yourself, why not?

Derek is a Mechanical Engineer with post-graduate degrees in Business Management, Environmental Science and Workplace Health & Safety. He has over 50 years of experience in heavy manufacturing, construction and maintenance management.

FOREWORD

BY DR S. SUBRAMANIAN

April 14th, 2021

Free Ice Cream. Who wouldn't want it? I was intrigued by the very idea espoused by Ganesh and read the entire book in one go.

Right from the Malthusian Trap of the 18th Century to the Club of Rome Report in 1972, we have all been conditioned to think of a world with just a finite set of resources – that we exist in a "zero-sum game environment". No wonder the phrase *there is no free lunch* strikes such a deep chord in all of us. It is this same ideology, this deeply-ingrained way of life we grew up with, that makes the concept of Free Ice Cream fascinating.

Given the complexity of this idea, Free Ice Cream could have either been daunting or a bore – or both. It could have been an amalgamation of scientific facts, infested with technical jargon and methods to accomplish zero costs.

Instead, Ganesh has made the book simple and easy to read. He gets heavy, scientific concepts across using basic business language. The writing draws the reader in with its colloquial, conversational style. Scientific thought is critical in today's world, and Ganesh manages to break the barrier that keeps it apart from everyday usage and comprehension. That is the mark of a truly intelligent, thoughtful writer.

Free Ice Cream talks to everyone – the artist, the technologist and the lay person, opening a world of endless opportunities to the reader. It is my belief that it will indeed be the business minded amongst us who will benefit the maximum from the conversations in Free Ice Cream.

The vision of an endlessly empowered and interconnected future with continuously shrinking and finally zero costs brings both challenges and benefits. But that ought to be the next book Ganesh should work on!

With a PhD in finance from the Indian Institute of Management, Ahmedabad, and over 32 years of experience, Dr S. Subramanian has led India's largest equity underwriter across the entire investment banking and equities spectrum.

BOOK 1

THE CONCEPT

The Brief

Mr. Mortimer turned around and addressed the class.

"For the Green, Blue and Yellow Groups, we will continue with the class for this term and you will have the end of year exams. The Orange group has delivered excellent grades so far. As such they will not have exams".

A groan went through the class. "It was not fair" seemed to be the general consensus among all students other than the Orange group, obviously.

"However", Mr. Mortimer continued, "The Orange group will complete a project in this term and will be graded based on the same".

Mr. Mortimer gently polished his glasses.

The class knew he was going to say something serious. For the last few terms, the students had watched and learned.

"How many of you like ice cream?" asked Mr. Mortimer.

Some hands went up.

"Well, how would it be if ice cream was free?"

There were smiles and nods across the class except the Orange group. "Where is he going with this", whispered Meg to Chen, her close friend. She didn't have to wait.

"Orange group, here is what I want you to do. I want you to open up an ice cream shop and give free ice creams to all who come to your shop. You will not charge your customers for the ice cream. The ice cream will be FREE".

"This is your project for this year. You have thirteen weeks to come up with a plan and convince me that it will work", said Mr. Mortimer.

On hearing this statement from Morty, there was deafening silence in class as the students slowly tried to take in this message. The Orange group members stood frozen with open jaws.

For the past two terms, the class had been doing Business Basics. They had been learning about how a business functions, about what is revenue, cost and profit. Today was the summary session.

Prior to this bomb shell, Morty was briefly touching upon all the aspects of Business they had learned over the last two terms. There was a presentation slide on the board that highlighted the key points.

- A business needs a purpose.
- A business can sell a product, a service or both.
- A business charges money for the product and/or service. This is the Revenue.
- A business incurs costs in making the product or providing the service.
- Profit is Revenue less cost.
- A business has to be profitable in order to survive.

A footnote on the board indicated that for a manufacturing business, the major costs would be cost of raw materials, cost of labour, cost of energy and cost of capital to build the factory. For a Service business, it was predominantly cost of labour.

"But Mr. Morty, how is that possible?" piped in Karan. "You have been telling us all year that a business cannot run without making a profit. If we give ice creams out for free where is the profit?"

Karan was a studious boy who was not well liked by most of the other kids. Meg was his only friend, if you could call it that.

"If we give it away for free, there is no revenue. Hence no profit", Chen said supporting Karan. Chen had enjoyed basic business and had gained a good understanding of the subject over the year.

Mr. Mortimer pulled up his pants.

The class knew he was going to say or do something outrageous. For the last few terms, the students had watched and learned. He was not called Mad Mortimer for nothing.

Mr. Mortimer cackled making a little dancing step and said, "You are right. But I will make an exception to the rule. I will give you energy for free to make your ice cream".

The Orange group stared back at him with a puzzled look. The bell went off. As the class rose to be dismissed, Mr. Mortimer said, "Every week we will catch up on this project. You will give me an update on what you have done, and you have thirteen weeks to go".

The walk back home was gloomy. "There goes my straight A's record", fumed Karan. "Why did mad Morty have to come up with something this weird?"

Meg had no come backs. For once, she seemed to be agreeing with Karan wholeheartedly.

CHAPTER 2

The Emperor

Nader was home. You could hear that noise from his room he called music.

Meg went to the fridge to grab a sandwich. The freezer beckoned. She did not want to look at the ice cream inside.

As she was sitting down with her sandwich, she could hear footsteps. The Emperor is coming down she thought. She rued the fact that her Dad was travelling on Work and her Mum was at work and will not be home for a while.

Rightly so, the Emperor emerged.

Nader was tall. He had shot up in the last couple of years. With his added height, he seemed to be looking down on others. Meg knew that it was not just the added height, but his whole attitude. For the past couple of years, he had been looking down on the lesser mortals.

"Hey, you down there", the Emperor addressed

the lowly being. "Why the gloom?"

Meg was in no mood for conversation with this apparition that used to be her brother. She kept munching the sandwich.

"You have been addressed. That means you need to respond", the Emperor stated.

Meg drew a long breath and said, "Nothing".

"Really. Then why do I think that you will be running in the Derby the coming weekend?"

Seeing Meg's confused look, the Emperor explained, "Why the long face?"

Meg had a flash of inspiration. "Morty's problem is going to really stuff him up", she thought. This is my chance. Let me throw it at him and enjoy the sight of the Emperor creeping back to his cave with his tail between his legs.

So, Meg explained the project that Morty had assigned them that day. When she came to the part of Morty providing them with free energy, Nader cracked up.

"That Morty, with his silly old tricks on the young, the ignorant and the gullible. I mean you and your friends of course", Nader stated just in case Meg hadn't got the jibe. "You guys are cannon fodder, for sure", he cackled.

Meg gave him a hard look.

"It is pretty simple", Nader explained. "Even you

know that everything in this world is made up of atoms and molecules. All you need to do is to pick up the right atoms and molecules and smash them together with Morty's free energy".

"Voila, Ice Cream!"

And with that explanation, the Emperor retreated to his royal abode upstairs.

CHAPTER 3

The Project Room

For the next Business Basics Class, the Orange group convened in the Project Room.

Mr. Mortimer had given the Orange group a Project Room adjacent to the library. He had explained that the group did not need to attend classes and could spend the Business Basics period in the Project Room.

For the first few minutes, there was silence in the room. No one seemed to want to say anything. Miya gently cleared her throat and said, "Any ideas anyone?"

"I think we should lodge a formal protest with the principal and get ourselves out of this project", Karan said. "We have been working our butts off the whole year and have gotten decent grades and is this our reward for that? To be penalized like this?" Karan was fuming.

"Why don't we at least give it a try before shooting

it down?" asked Emma.

"Because it goes against everything that we have been taught this year. Have you been sleeping through the year or what?" Karan retorted.

Emma gently retreated.

"Maybe this is about thinking out of the box", Chen said. "I agree with Karan that this goes against all that we have been taught this year. So, how about we start looking at this problem from outside of business basics?"

"Like what?" Karan was still in a fighting mood.

"OK. Who does things for free?" responded Chen.

"The Salvos give things for free. Bread, soup, why not ice cream?" Emma responded.

Karan gave her a scornful look and said, "They are a charity. We are talking about a business".

"So, let us make our ice cream shop a charity. We can give free ice creams to all", Emma said. There was a general murmur in the group. Everyone seemed to think of it as a good idea.

"Ok. That is one idea worth pursuing. What else?" said Chen. With continued silence in the group, Chen continued, "The UN does a lot of work in various countries and I don't think they charge for what they do. Why not explore that model and use it for our ice cream shop?"

"How is that different from charity?" asked Karan.

"I don't know. But it might be worth exploring", said Chen.

Karan seemed to be getting back in the groove and said, "If we are going to be looking at this kind of stuff, maybe we can explore things like crowd funding as well where we raise funds through social media and run our ice cream shop on that".

"Really? Will that model work?" asked Chen.

"I don't know. But it might be worth exploring", responded Karan with a cheeky smile.

Meg was taking it all in and had not opened her mouth during the conversation.

Presently there was a knock on the door and Morty entered. The group hadn't realized that the hour was almost up.

"How is it going guys?" asked Morty.

"Not very well", responded Miya. "Mr. Morty, this project seems to be going against all that we have learned this year in Business Basics. So, we are exploring things outside the box, as Chen puts it".

"Interesting", replied Morty, "what have you come up with?"

"Well, not much really. One option is to establish the ice cream shop as a charity. That way we can give free ice cream to all".

The group was watching Morty carefully for his reaction. Morty pursed his lips, emitted a longish hum.

"We are also considering models similar to what the UN does", Karan chipped in, "and we also want to explore options like crowd funding using social media", concluded Chen.

"Another option is to sell other things in this shop and charge for them. That revenue may offset the loss due to free ice cream", said Miya. The rest of the group looked at her with some interest as this was off-the-cuff.

Morty continued to keep looking at them and it looked like the group had nothing more to table. The silence was weighing down on them.

Meg did not want to table Nader's atom smash solution, but the awkward silence did it for her. Meg cleared her throat and said, "Mr. Morty, we know that ice cream is made of atoms and molecules. With your free energy, we might be able to smash atoms to make free ice cream".

"Excellent", Morty said with a big smile on his face. "But why do I get the feeling that you are not sold on this idea yourself?" he asked Meg, "Are you?"

"Yes and No", said Meg. "Scientifically it is feasible I suppose, but I was not sure if you were looking for this as a solution".

"So, how is the Emperor? Still looking down on us lowly peasants?" queried Morty smiling at Meg. Morty could infer that the atom smash idea most likely came from Nader who had been his student a few years back and had been a big proponent of atom smash solutions for all problems.

"It is good that you guys are exploring alternate options", continued Morty addressing the whole group.

"Allow me to clarify", Mr. Mortimer gently polished his glasses.

"No. The ice cream shop will not be a charity, government funded or crowd funded.

And no, the ice cream shop will not sell other products to offset the loss".

Morty continued, "Business Basics rules will still apply. If you borrow funding, you need to return it. Cost, revenue and profit are the key parameters you can play with, and most importantly, it will have to be a business that is sustainable".

The group knew what a sustainable business was. The business had to survive on its own. They could not get any money to run the business from other people or the government. The only money they could get was from the revenue by selling their ice cream.

"And any solution that you come up with has to be something that is being done today or should be something that can be done in the near future. I do not want science fiction solutions. So, atom smash is out", Morty was smiling at Meg as he said it.

Morty continued, "It is obvious that if you are

going to be giving free ice cream, your revenue is zero. Therefore, the only option is to make the cost zero as well. Correct?"

Heads nodded in agreement.

"Here is my tip. Why don't you go out there and figure out what are the costs in an ice cream factory? That might be a good place to start".

On that high note, Morty tipped his imaginary hat and left the room.

CHAPTER 4

Yossi

The group trudged over to the ice cream shop. Chen ambled up to the counter and said, "We would like to talk to the owner". The girl at the counter looked puzzled.

"Is there an issue with the ice cream?" she queried.

"No. Not really", Chen responded. "You see, we have been given a project at school. We want to talk to the owner and get some information about the shop".

"Yossi, there's some kids to see you", the girl sang to the back of the shop.

A big man came from the back of the shop. Chen gathered he must be Yossi.

"What's up kids?" he said. "How can I help you?"

"Sir, we have been given a project at school about an ice cream shop. We thought you might be able to help us. Would you have some time for us?"

"Sure. Come back into my office", replied Yossi.

The office was a little room at the back of the shop. Yossi plonked himself in his chair behind the desk and said, "Shoot".

"Our teacher has given us this project where we will have to open up an ice cream shop and give free ice creams to all who come to the shop", Chen said and hastily added, "not for real you know. Just as a presentation".

Yossi let out a big belly laughter that rang on for a while. "Oh, you got one of those have you? I had a teacher just like that back in school", he guffawed. "But this one takes the cake, or should I say ice cream", Yossi beamed.

Meg could see Yossi liked what he considered his sense of wit.

"Free indeed. Really?" Yossi was still beaming. "Wonder where they come up with these ideas. By the way what class is this project for?"

"Well sir, it is our project for Business Basics", Meg replied.

Yossi stopped beaming. His eyebrows knotted up and he seemed perplexed. "Business Basics is a class you take in school? What do they teach you?"

"So far, we have learned about revenue, cost, profit and things like that", said Meg.

"Mmmm, I think I understand why you have been given this project. Good one too", Yossi unknotted his eyebrows. "It is a good way to learn how nothing is for free".

"Okay, here is the deal", Yossi continued, "I am happy to help you guys. However, we will need to spend some time on this for what I have in mind".

Yossi pondered for a while and said, "Why don't you guys come over on ..." Yossi started flicking through his diary. "How about tomorrow? You come over and we will spend a couple of hours. I can explain how we make our ice cream and you guys might be able to finish your project".

As they walked back, Chen said, "Are you sure this is what Morty wanted, to say that nothing is free".

"But then, throughout the year that is what Morty has been drilling into us. So, he better accept our presentation that nothing is free", Meg fumed.

So, what was that comment about energy being free, they wondered?

CHAPTER 5

The Ice Cream Factory

"Welcome guys", Yossi beamed. Looked like he was back to his jovial self.

"Let us gear up", he said and took them to the locker behind his office. He handed them white coats that looked like lab coats and hair nets. "Hygiene is very important in a food factory. We do not want any contamination of the product", he explained.

Once they were geared up, Yossi led them into the factory. The place was humming with various shiny machines in operation. There were a few people decked up like themselves working around the machines. The place was cold.

"Let us start from the back, shall we?", Yossi said. The group trudged along following Yossi to the back of the factory.

There was a shed and some shiny tanks at the back. "Milk, cream and liquid sugar come in tankers and gets pumped into these tanks. We then pump these into the mixing tank at the right proportions".

"How do they get mixed?" queried Chen.

"You look at that thing on top of the tank. That is a motor that turns the shaft and paddle inside the mixing tank", explained Yossi.

"By the way that compressor over there", Yossi pointed to a machine just outside the factory, "is the one that freezes the ice cream".

They walked further, and Yossi pointed to a big shiny box that was humming. "That is the homogenizer". Looking at the blank stares from the kids, he explained, "Well, that machine mixes the fat and milk, so they don't separate".

"And this is the pasteurizer. Here we heat up the mixture to get rid of any pathogens. That way, the ice cream is safe for you and will not make you sick".

Karan was furiously making notes. Yossi had clearly spelled out the rules. No photos or videos of the factory.

"And the ice cream mixture gets cooled here. We then send it to the ice cream maker", Yossi kept pointing at various machines. There were pipes going in and out of these machines with ice built up on them.

At the end of the ice cream maker, the kids could see ice cream oozing out of a spout and was filling little tubs. "That is the conveyor that brings empty tubs and moves them on once they are filled", Yossi explained. A little machine put the lid on the tubs that were being stacked on a shelf by some people. "The stacked shelves go into the freezer", Yossi pointed out to a sealed room further up.

"Let us get back to the office", Yossi said and led them back to the locker where they removed their hair nets and coats.

While going into the office, Yossi turned around and asked, "Who would like to have a free ice cream?" All heads nodded. Yossi went up to a nearby freezer and opened it up. "Take your pick", he said.

Once they had helped themselves to a cup each, they went into the office.

"So, what do you think?"

"Loved it", Emma piped up. "I always thought factories were dirty places but this one is so clean. How come all of your machines are so shiny?"

"This is a food factory and cleanliness and hygiene are critical. Just about all the machines are made of stainless steel so they do not corrode even when wet".

Once in the office Yossi plonked himself in the chair.

"Now that you have seen it, can you explain to me how ice cream is made", Yossi queried.

"Well, you get the milk, cream and sugar and put them through the machines to make ice cream. You then pack them in tubs with your packing machine", Emma said.

"Well, that is a pretty good summary of what we do even though I wish you hadn't made it look so simple", Yossi smiled. "But there is one flaw. You see, we don't get our milk, cream and sugar. We buy them from our suppliers, meaning we pay for them".

"And that is the first cost to my business", Yossi continued. "Then of course I have to pay my people in the factory. And don't forget the power bill to run all the machines". Yossi's smile was fading at the thought of all the money he was paying out.

"And then I have my dear bank who expects their money back"; looking at the puzzled looks, Yossi explained, "You see all these machines cost a lot of money. So, I go to the bank, take a loan to buy the machines and set up this factory. Obviously, I have to pay the money back to the bank, with interest, don't I?"

"With all these costs, I will have to sell the ice cream at a price where I can make a profit and not go broke".

"So, how do you expect me to give away ice cream for free? Can you please explain, because I am REALLY interested to know", Yossi's hands were open and was beckoning the group to provide him with the magical answer.

The group remained silent.

"Look, I will not share my numbers with you", Yossi clarified, "I mean my actual business revenue, cost and profit". "But I will help you with some indicative numbers for a tub of ice cream and you can use that for your presentation. Okay?"

Heads nodded.

"So, assume, to make one tub of ice cream, I spend one dollar on milk, cream and sugar, another dollar on paying all of my people, say fifty cents on my power bills and another fifty cents to the bank to pay back on my loan for the machines. Where does that leave me?"

"Three dollars a tub", Karan replied in a monotone.

"Well, Mr. Morty said he would give power for free", Emma chipped in.

"Oh, very generous of him", Yossi wasn't smiling, but he completely ignored Emma's comment and carried on. "So, it costs me three dollars. If I sell a tub for, say, three dollars and fifty cents, I make a profit of fifty cents. Sounds right?" Yossi queried.

The group nodded.

"This way I sustain my business. I don't go broke and am able to feed my family and please, please, don't get me started on the tax I end up paying on the profit", Yossi groaned.

"So, kids, your teacher was right. You have come

to a real business in the real world and this is how things work here. There is no such thing as free ice cream".

The walk back from the ice cream factory was anything but cheerful.

CHAPTER 6

Ambush Morty

The next day, as the group moved towards the canteen, Meg said, "Look, let us have a chat with Morty and hopefully he will agree with the work we have done so far. We can then complete that and get it out of the way".

Chen seemed to agree by nodding. Karan did not respond, and Emma said, "I doubt it. But let's give it a try".

At the Canteen, they could see Morty sitting by himself having his lunch. The group approached him.

"Mr. Morty, can we have a few minutes sir?" Meg opened.

"Yes, what about?" Morty responded.

"It is about the project Sir", Meg continued. "We went to the ice cream factory and had a chat with the owner. He even took us around and explained how they made ice cream".

"That is good effort guys. Well done", Morty said.

"Yossi also explained what his costs were and how he will have to sell it at a certain price to cover his costs and make a profit", Meg blurted.

"He even gave us some indicative revenue, cost and profit figures that we can use for the project. He said he cannot give his actual figures", Chen added.

"So, looks like the ice cream has a price and is not free", Morty was smiling.

"Sir, Yossi said that there is no such thing as free ice cream. He even mentioned that maybe you have given us this project just to prove that", Emma piped in.

Mr. Mortimer gently polished his glasses.

"Sit down kids", he said. They pulled up some chairs and sat down.

Morty searched for something in his phone. He then turned it around and asked them, "What do you see?"

It was a picture of a parrot.

"What is special about this bird?"

"Well, they are colourful and beautiful", Emma replied.

"Did you know that they can be trained to repeat whatever we tell them?" Morty asked. Some did know of this and nodded. Chen had an inkling of what was to come and wished he hadn't come along.

"So, I taught you something in class and you come

back to me repeating the same thing even when I asked you to do otherwise".

Morty continued, "You see, I do not want to raise a bunch of parrots. I would like to see you guys think for yourselves and show me that I have been wrong. And that is going to require some more effort from you guys".

The group was silent. The message was clear. The door to the easy way out had been slammed.

"I can understand you getting stuck at this juncture", Morty said. "So, here is a tip. Why don't you go and have a chat with the professor on the hill?"

The professor had been mentioned, in passing, in the past. Morty assured the group that he will talk to the professor and get him to meet the group the next day.

CHAPTER 7

Prof. Iyer

The bus dropped them off at the stop at the base of the hill. The hill wasn't too steep but had no paved road or steps going up. Just a dirt track that was probably good enough for a truck.

The walk up was not too onerous. It was a beautiful day with a mild cool breeze. The group reached the shack at the top of the hill and rang the bell.

"Yello", a voice from inside rang out. Presently the front door opened, and a tall lanky man appeared. Meg looked at his shocking white head of hair and concluded that the man had given up combing his hair for a long time.

"You must be the students Morty was talking about", the person smiled. "I am Professor Iyer. Well, come on in".

The group trudged behind Prof. Iyer.

"So, what is up? Morty said you guys wanted to have a chat with me", Iyer said.

"Well Professor, it is like this", Emma started and explained the project and the quandary to Prof. Iyer.

Prof. Iyer gave out a big smile. "So, Morty said Energy is free, did he?" he beamed. "That was clever of him to give that hint. Why do you think he said that?"

The group became silent. Chen was squirming inside, and he blurted out, "It was something that was nagging me throughout, professor. But talking to Yossi at the ice cream factory, the energy was only one part of the cost. He still had to pay for the milk, cream and sugar, pay for the machines in the factory and pay the people working there. So, even if we took out the cost of energy, there is still a lot of costs and how are we going to make the ice cream free?"

"I think that was very well put", Prof. Iyer commented. "You know why, because you have stated your problem so well that the solution is right there".

Chen was puzzled but maintained his silence.

"Obviously I can't give you the solution, but I can guide you in the right way. So, here is my tip", Prof. Iyer continued.

"The raw materials, machines and labour cost money, right?"

Heads nodded.

"You have two options", the professor continued, "One, you can get rid of them and make your ice cream without them or you can find out why they cost money and find a way to make them free".

Prof. Iyer wrapped with the comment, "The most valuable advice I can give you at this point in time is – Keep Digging".

Walking down the hill, Miya opened up, "Can't make ice cream without the ingredients, can we?"

"Well, we could replace the machines and do it all by hand. No Machines. Handmade Ice Cream!! That will be a good sales pitch", beamed Chen.

"And that will mean more people", smirked Meg. Chen's face clouded.

"You know what. I think we can get rid of the people. We can automate the whole factory and we will not need any people", Karan popped up.

"Well, that means more machines, right?" Chen shot back.

"Maybe, but at least that is one less problem. This way we only have to worry about two and not three", Karan retorted.

The cranky group boarded the bus to get back to town.

CHAPTER 8

The Search

The group convened at the Project Room the next day.

"We either eliminate or liberate", Emma said dreamily. Looking at the puzzled looks around, she said, "What's tripping you up?"

"Eliminate, ok but liberate? Really? What is this, a project on slavery?" Karan looked mildly irritated.

"Liberate from the burden of cost of course", shot back Emma. "Where's the poet in you? Of course, you are the terminator who will eliminate all people and send them home with no jobs".

"At least I focus on something other than a so-called catchy slogan", Karan retorted.

Meg was watching Miya while the rest of the group was bickering. Miya seemed thoughtful.

"Any bright ideas?" Meg asked Miya. Miya didn't seem to take offence at the tone and instead replied, "Looks like our best option is to follow the thread to the end".

This seemed to cause more confusion.

"If we assume that the factory can be automated", Miya paused, looking inquiringly at Karan. Karan seemed to nod affirmatively. "Then we will have to figure out why the machines and ingredients cost money? Right?"

Heads nodded in agreement as Miya continued, "Why don't we split as teams and chase it up?"

"How are we going to chase it up?" Karan piped up.

"I don't know. Maybe we go and ask some people for a start", Miya responded.

"I don't think we will get anything more from the hill", Chen said.

Meg intervened, "Let us try other avenues. I will start off with my parents. Maybe they will tell us something or maybe they will know of someone who can help. Suggest you guys do the same as well. Let us exchange notes tomorrow".

Meg walked back with Emma and could see Emma was upset. She knew it was Karan's idea of automating the factory to get rid of people.

"It's okay Emma. This is only a project", Meg said.

Emma slowly turned to Meg and said, "Not really Meg. Early this year my dad was laid off because they brought in some robots to do his work. It took him a while to find another job. Things were not happy at home till he found the new job. I just hate this idea of factory with no people".

Meg squeezed Emma's hand as they continued to walk.

CHAPTER 9

The Collation

The group convened at the Project Room three days later. Meg had indicated that she had something to share.

Meg got the group around her and said, "Look, I spent some time with my neighbour who is an engineer. He gave me a lot of information on how machines are made. I think I will keep the details aside", Meg waved the notebook and continued, "and just provide a brief summary for the project. We can always provide the details later, as a footnote, if Morty wants it".

The group nodded in agreement.

"A machine is typically made of various components assembled together. The components are mostly made of different types of metals. Man-made synthetic materials like plastics, rubber, foam, etc. also come in to play.

For our project, we will just focus on metal and

plastic as raw materials to make machine components.

We typically heat or cool the metal or plastic with energy sources like electricity or gas. We then use machines to pound, cut or shape the metal or plastic material into components", said Meg.

"So, we use energy and machines to convert the raw material into components. Correct?" asked Chen.

"True", replied Meg and continued, "We then use other machines and people to assemble the components and make the machine that we want. By the way, all these component-making machines and people are located in a place called the factory".

As Meg finished, Karan said, "I think that is a good start. I'm sure you have enough information to support your summary in that notebook. But the bigger question is how does this help us with free ice cream?"

The group nodded in agreement and was still confused about where this was all leading to.

Miya said, "Look, let us follow Prof. Iyer on this. He said keep digging, right?"

Chen put his hand up and said, "Look, just to clarify what Meg said. We need metal and plastic as raw materials to make machines. Correct?"

The group agreed.

Chen continued, "So, we need to find out how metal and plastic are made in the first place".

The group agreed. Karan put his hand up to find out how metals are made. Following up on her successful run with finding out how machines are made, Meg volunteered to find out how plastics are made.

"We still need to figure out the story behind the ingredients for ice cream, milk, cream and sugar", Miya said.

Chen fancied himself as an expert on farming. He had once visited a rice farm in his ancestral Cambodia when he had gone for a visit with his parents. He offered to chase up the story behind ingredients. Miya said, "I will work with Chen and we will get some information on that".

Metal and Plastic

The group convened at the Project Room the next week. Meg and Karan had information to share.

Karan kicked off the session. "Guys, I spoke to a company that deals with metals. The lady there gave me a lot of information on the various steps involved in making metals. Taking Meg's cue, I will provide a brief summary for this project. I still have the details and we can present if Morty wants that information", said Karan.

Karan continued, "It looks like metal is present underground as ore. You dig the ore out, grind it and then clean the ore. This is the mining process. We then heat up the clean ore and melt it to make whatever metal you want. We can even mix different metals to make new metals called alloys.

You need machines to do all this digging, grinding, cleaning activities. You also need energy to run the machines and people to operate the machines. But for this project, we can automate everything and make it people-free", Karan reported to the group.

"And Morty is giving us free energy. So, the only thing we need to worry about is how to make these machines free", said Chen.

Emma said, "Karan, you keep talking about automating everything. Then what will the people do for jobs?"

"Not my problem", replied Karan.

"Really?"

"Well, factory automation is happening even now. Robots are in factories as we speak. Trust me, I have done one complete semester on Artificial intelligence (AI) last year", said Karan.

"That is great. But you still haven't answered my question", said Emma.

"Look Emma, Business Basics clearly spells out that Labour is a cost. We are trying to get rid of cost for this project. If you have a better solution ..." Karan did not finish the sentence.

He did not have to. Emma retreated in silence.

Meg gently cleared her throat and said, "I think this issue of job losses needs to be discussed. Maybe we do not need to do it right now, but we should address this".

Karan said, "Fine. If anyone has any bright ideas let us hear that. I am only promoting this for the project because it works, and no one has offered any other alternative".

With no response from the group, Karan asked Meg for an update on how plastics are made.

Meg said, "I had a good discussion with my aunt who is a petrochemical engineer. She explained to me how plastics are made. Interestingly, it does not seem very different to how metals are made".

"It is a four-step process. You drill and extract crude oil. You then heat it up and cool it to extract whatever hydrocarbon you want. You then heat up different hydrocarbons in the presence of a catalyst and cool them to make plastic. Then you heat up the plastic, pour into moulds and cool it to make the plastic component you want".

"You need machines to do all this drilling, refining and manufacturing activities. You also need energy to run the machines and people to operate the machines".

"Time out. Let me see if I have got this right", Chen said. "To make metal or plastic, you need machines to do various activities. You also need energy to run the machines and people to operate the machines".

"But for this project, we can automate everything and make it people-free and Morty is giving us free energy. So, the only thing we need to worry about is how to make these machines free", said Chen.

The group seemed to be in agreement on this.

CHAPTER 11

The Paradox

Meg turned to Miya and Chen and asked, "Any info on how the ice cream raw materials are made?"

Miya said, "Look there is a lot to share. Let us tell you the story and then we can decide what to present".

Chen and Miya took turns on telling their story, their visit to the Milk Farm, to the Sugarcane Farm and to the Sugar Mill. It was captivating and interesting.

At the end of the story, Miya summarized, "Interestingly, the Milk Farm has a lot of machines which all need energy to run and some people to operate the machines. The Milk Farm also needs feed for the cows which is mostly organic matter like silage, grass, hay, cottonseeds and the like. However, the feed is a major cost for them".

Chen said, "The Sugarcane Farm scenario is not any different. They have farming machines that need energy to run and some people to operate the machines. For them, the main cost seems to be water and fertilizer".

Chen continued, "The Sugar Mill is just another factory. They have a bunch of machines to squeeze the juice out of the sugarcane. There are other machines to heat up the juice and produce sugar. All the machines in the mill need people to operate the machines. Interestingly, energy is not a cost as they make their own electricity and are carbon neutral too".

"It looks like it is the same story everywhere, machines, energy and people. Every activity seems to require machines to make things as well as energy and people to run the machines", commented Emma.

Meg pondered aloud, "With free energy and automated factories, two of the cost items are eliminated. Ok. But what do we do with the machines?"

"You need metals and plastic to make machines in the first place?" said Chen.

"But you need machines to make the metals and plastic in the first place", observed Miya.

"How do you get out of this chicken and egg paradox?" asked Emma.

The group pondered over this for a while. With no light bulbs popping over anyone's head, Miya took a deep breath and said, "Looks like we are staring at a brick wall. Why don't we take a walk up the hill?"

The group nodded in agreement gloomily.

CHAPTER 12

The Hill Climb

Prof. Iyer was slouched on his couch.

Meg kicked it off saying, "Prof. Iyer, I think we have done a fair amount of work. Now we understand how metal and plastics are made, how machines are made".

Prof. Iyer stayed slouched on his couch, but his eyebrows beckoned Meg to continue. Meg gave him a brief summary of progress so far.

"Excellent", responded Prof. Iyer. "That is good progress. So, what next?" he queried.

"Well Prof, Morty is giving us free energy. So, that is not a problem. We can also automate all machines. So, the people cost is eliminated as well. That leaves us with machines. How do we make them free?" asked Karan.

"We have found out that you need metals and plastic to make machines. But you need machines to make the metals and plastic in the first place. Isn't this a Catch-22 situation?" queried Miya.

Prof. Iyer drew a long breath and pondered for a while. He then asked, "Do you guys really believe that things can be made for free".

The group remained silent.

"Thought so", continued Prof. Iyer. "You guys do not believe that this is possible. Right?"

There was no response from the group.

"You see, if you don't believe it to be possible, you will not be motivated to find a solution. You will treat every obstacle as if it is the end of the road. You will not look at the obstacle as something to be overcome to achieve your goal".

"And it is not your fault", continued Prof. Iyer. "It is just the environment that you live in. Everybody has been telling you that it is not possible. In the last few weeks, I am sure people have told you, repeatedly, that nothing is for free. Right?"

Heads nodded.

"And you have all watched your parents go to work every day to get money, so you can buy things. The message has gone hard and deep into you. You must pay for everything. Nothing is for free".

"So, I am going to tell you a little story. Let us say I give you a rooster and ten hens". He paused for a while and said, "I think that ratio might be just about right".

The Prof. continued, "You have them in your backyard. Now the hens start laying eggs. In a month, every hen would have hatched say ten chickens. So, now, you have hundred chickens. Half of them would be male and the other half female. You keep all the fifty female chicks which will grow up to be egg laying hens in about six months' time.

You also keep say five male chicks which will grow up to be productive roosters. You can give away the rest. Clear so far?" the Prof. queried.

Heads nodded.

"In six months' time, the chicks will have grown up and be ready to reproduce; the fifty chicks would now be hens and will start laying eggs.

At that point in time, you give me back my rooster and ten hens.

So, now you have fifty hens and five roosters that is all yours. You start giving away some eggs and chickens for free while you continue to hatch some eggs to continue to grow your flock.

How does that sound?"

"What about the cost of chicken feed and water for the chickens?" queried Emma.

"If we consider Feed and Water as fuel for Chickens, then it is Morty's responsibility, isn't it? He said he will give you fuel for free", replied Prof. Iyer.

"But this is farming, not manufacturing with

machines", retorted Karan.

"Well, it is an analogy. As with all analogies, this one is also not perfect. However, you might start thinking along these lines for your solution", replied Prof. Iyer.

The walk down the hill was lively. Suddenly the group seemed to be fired up. Everyone seemed to have an opinion on how the chicken story was going to contribute to their project.

Arriving at the bottom of the hill, the group parked themselves at the bus stop waiting for the bus into town.

Miya was craning her neck and looking into the road when she said, "I think I get it".

"What?" was the chorus response.

"I think the rooster and hens are our factories. I think Prof. Iyer is telling us to have factories that make machines to make other factories".

"But why?" responded Karan.

"Let us go back", said Miya.

And they all trudged up the hill again.

CHAPTER 13

The Dialogue

"That was fast", said Prof. Iyer.

"Well, Prof. Iyer, we started discussing your chicken story going down the hill. We think the rooster and hens are our factories. So, we will need to have a machine-making factory that will make machines to create all other factories", said Miya.

"Very good take", commented Prof. Iyer. "Now how is this going to help you?" asked Prof. Iyer.

"We may need some guidance on that", said Emma.

"OK. Let us think this through", said Prof. Iyer.

"You have free energy for the ice cream factory. Correct?" asked Prof. Iyer.

"Yes", the group responded.

"Let us say you automate the whole factory, hence no people either", said Prof. Iyer.

"Yes", the group responded.

"So, the only thing you need is the machines to

make ice cream?" said Prof. Iyer.

"No", said the group. "We also need raw materials for the ice cream like milk, cream and sugar".

"OK, let us park the ice cream raw materials for a moment and continue. We will come back to it later. Now take me through the process of how you will make free ice cream–making machines", said Prof. Iyer.

Prof. Iyer continued, "Let me give you a machine-making factory that can make all kinds of machines, the first hen so to speak. What can you do with this?" asked Prof. Iyer.

"With your factory, we will first make the machines required to build another machine-making factory, same as hens making more hens", responded Meg and continued, "We will build the second machine-making factory and give the first factory back to you. The second factory that we build will be fully automated and Morty will provide free energy to run it".

"We now have a machine-making factory that is free of cost. Correct?" asked Meg.

"Not exactly. You have borrowed the metal and plastic required to make your own machine-making factory. You will continue to borrow these raw materials for any other machines that you make in your factory", said Prof. Iyer.

"So, our next step obviously is to see how to make

the raw materials free", said Chen.

"Spot on", said Prof. Iyer and asked, "Based on your research, what are the steps to making metal?"

"You dig the ore out, grind it and then clean the ore. This is the mining process. We then heat up the clean ore and melt it to make whatever alloy or metal you want", said Karan.

"And ..." prompted Prof. Iyer.

Karan had a light-bulb moment.

"In our machine-making factory, we will first start making mining machines, machines to dig the ore out, grind it and then clean the ore.

We will then make machines to build a metal factory, machines that heat up the clean ore and melt it to make whatever metal we want. Our machines will be fully automated. With free energy from Morty, the metal that we produce is free. Right?" asked Karan.

"Bingo", said Prof. Iyer.

It was slowly dawning on the group that there was actually a way out of this maze.

"I think we can take the same approach to plastics as free raw material as well?" said Meg.

"Looks like you are on a roll", said Prof. Iyer and continued, "So, now we have free raw materials to make any machine that we want. What do you think you will want to make next?" asked Prof. Iyer.

"Ice cream–making machines", the group responded

in unison.

"Aren't you jumping ahead of yourself?" asked Prof. Iyer.

There was general confusion. What had they missed?

"Sure, you can now make ice cream–making machines and build a fully automated ice cream factory. But what about the raw materials for making ice cream like milk, cream and sugar? Have you made them free yet?" asked Prof. Iyer.

Having got the essence of the approach so far, Miya jumped in and said, "The cane farm needs machines to plant and harvest the crop. It also needs water and fertilizer for the crops".

"At our machine-making factory, we will make all automated farming machinery for the cane farm. We will also make water pumps to bring water to the cane farm", said Chen.

"Next we will make machines to build a fertilizer factory. The minerals and hydrocarbons needed for making the fertilizer will be sourced from our mines and our oil and gas factories", said Meg.

"So, at this point, we have all the costs eliminated for the Sugarcane Farm. So, the sugarcane is free. Correct?" asked Chen.

"Correct. Excellent", beamed Prof. Iyer and continued, "Chen, it was interesting that you mentioned making pumps to bring water to the farm. Do you think there is enough fresh water for everyone?"

Miya slapped her forehead and uttered, "Desalination".

Chen looked crestfallen as he hadn't thought of it first and lamely finished, "We will make machines to build fully automated desalination plants. With free energy, we will have free fresh water for everyone".

Miya said, "Now that we have made sugarcane free, let us focus on the Milk Farm".

Chen said, "The Milk Farm needs machines and feed for the cows which is mostly organic matter like silage, grass, hay, cottonseeds and the like".

Miya said, "At our machine-making factory, we will make all automated machinery for the Milk Farm".

"And we will have drones herding the cows", said Chen who was always very fond of this idea.

"That leaves us with the cost of feed", said Miya.

"Hold on", cried Emma, "If we can grow sugarcane for free, why can't we grow grass or other feed for free as well?"

"Bingo", yelled Chen, "Now feed cost is eliminated. So, we have the milk and cream from the Milk Farm free as well".

"Our machine-making factory will also make fully automated transport trucks to bring the milk and cream to the ice cream factory", piped in Karan.

Prof. Iyer had an amused look on his face noticing how all of the kids seemed to have missed the enormity of Emma's statement, including Emma.

Prof. Iyer let it go and said, "Who wants to summarize?"

Miya responded saying, "We borrow a machine-making factory from you and build our own machine-making factory. We then make machines to get free metal, follow a similar process to get free plastic and then start making machines that we need like farm machinery, machines for the Sugar Mill, desalination machines for free water, pumps, milking machines, transport machines and ice cream–making machines. We can then make free ice cream".

"Is that a wrap?" asked Prof. Iyer indicating that they had a solution.

"Prof. Iyer, there is still one issue here", Emma opened up. "Mr. Morty only said he will give us free energy. He never said anything about giving us a machine-making factory for free. There is also the issue of giving us metal and plastic for free till we build our factories and start making our own free metal and plastic", said Emma.

"Could it be because you never asked", smiled Prof. Iyer, "and when you ask Morty, I think you can expect him to throw a curveball", he cautioned. "I certainly would", continued Prof. Iyer, "because your solution can be much more elegant and holistic than this and the beauty is that you are almost there".

CHAPTER 14

The Curveball

"Listen guys, we just can't go to Mr. Morty and blurt out what we want", Miya was clear in her message to the group, "especially with the curveball that Prof. Iyer referred to".

"We are almost there with the solution he wanted. We do not want any curveballs at this point. We just need a little help from him with the first factory and some raw materials".

Meg thought Miya would fit well in politics.

"Let us manage this situation carefully and not blow it. We need to prepare and present a good story on how we have arrived at the solution, how much effort we have put to get here and then gently tell him that, by the way, we will also need a few other things to get us started".

The group agreed. It was worth putting in the effort to soften Mr. Morty before asking for more. They did some practice runs on presenting a well-streamed story with each person taking turns. They had scheduled some time with Mr. Morty in the afternoon during lunch break.

Over lunch break, they went up to Mr. Morty's room and started presenting their story. Mr. Morty seemed very pleased on hearing their presentation. He kept mumbling "excellent" many times as the story progressed.

On close of their presentation, as agreed, Emma stepped up and said, "Mr. Mortimer, as you can see, we have come up with a solution to give free ice creams to all. However, we will also need a machine-making factory and raw materials for free till we can start making our own metal and plastics".

Mr. Mortimer frowned for a while pondering this request and suddenly broke into a big smile. "Of course, you guys have done great work and I should permit this. So, let us say I will give you a machine-making factory and raw materials for free".

The group broke into a loud cheer.

Mr. Mortimer pulled up his pants. Noticing this, the group froze.

They knew he was going to say or do something outrageous.

Mr. Mortimer made a little dancing step and said, "I will give you a machine-making factory and raw materials for free, but only for a limited period, say ten years. You need to return my factory and raw materials by then. Ok?"

The group readily agreed, for this had been their plan in the first place. The mention of a timeframe changed nothing.

Mr. Mortimer continued, "Further, I will also limit free energy to only ten years", he paused and reiterated the point to make sure it was driven home well, "There will be no more free energy after ten years".

"And I want free ice creams for all, forever", Mr. Mortimer made a ballet-like step while uttering this. "And your project presentation is due in three days", Mr. Mortimer concluded.

He was certainly not the most popular person with the group at that point in time.

CHAPTER 15

The Sixer

Walking through the various classes for the rest of the day was painful for everyone. There was anger, frustration, a feeling of despair and anger again at getting the goalpost shifted so late in the project.

After the last class, with no previous plans to meet, the group gravitated to the project room. The first few minutes could be described as a pure rant and rave session with some members of the group bouncing off walls.

"How dare he" and "how can he do this" seemed to be the topic of discussion, if you could call that discussion. Someone suggested the hill and the rest of the group gave that person a very dark look that seemed to imply that "The hill got us here in the first place".

Miya put her hand up and said, "Guys, listen. All of us are very upset about the turn of events. Me too. Let us keep in mind that the hill referred to this and now Morty has done this to us. I have a strange feeling that the solution is right under our nose". The group was sceptical about this. However, it helped them to start thinking of a possible solution.

Miya continued, "Let us also keep in mind that we have prepared nothing so far. Whatever we have done is all in our heads. So, I propose that tomorrow we all sit down, agree on who presents what and start pulling information to put it together".

"To present on what", Karan's voice was a tad high pitched. "We don't have a solution yet", he said.

Miya replied, "It doesn't change the fact that we got so far and have done so much work. Look, worst-case scenario is we present on all that we have done and learned. I am sure we should still get good grades for our work".

"And if we present nothing, we won't be graded. We get nothing", concluded Chen.

The group agreed to start working on the presentation the next day.

That evening at home Meg's aunt had come home with her daughter Meher. The young girl was fond of Meg and Meg liked playing with her.

Meher opened a little bag of toys and pulled out a set of cards. Meg looked and realized they were sequence cards that depicted a range of pictures that could be arranged in the correct order for the picture story to make sense.

Meg shuffled the cards and laid them out. In the cards, Meg could see two girls looking up a fruit tree, getting a ladder to climb up the tree, pluck a couple of fruits, climb down and sit under the tree enjoying the fruits.

Meher was slowly moving the picture cards around with her little tongue sticking out. Meg was gently prompting Meher with some questions when her Labrador pup darted in and grabbed one of the cards. Meg went after him playing his game, cornered him and gently retrieved the card in one piece.

As she wiped and straightened the card, the realization hit her. She slapped her forehead and exclaimed. "Oh my God!"

Realizing she had startled young Meher, Meg pacified her saying, "It's ok Meher. You are doing well. Keep going. I'll be back in a moment".

Meg got her phone and sent out a message to the group: "WE BUILD THE POWER PLANT FIRST AND THEN THE REST IN SEQUENCE". Within moments responses varied from "WHAT?" to "BRILLIANT" to "OF COURSE" from group members.

The Preparation

The group was present in the project room and were animated with high fives flowing around.

Miya called the group to order.

"OK guys, let us start", she said.

"Wait", said Chen, "Let me also put some visuals together as we go. That will help us in putting the presentation together".

The group thought it was a good idea.

Meg kicked it off saying, "We borrow a machine-making factory from Morty and build our own fully automated machine-making factory. This factory will be able to make all kinds of machines. We will need raw materials to make these machines and we will borrow the raw materials from Morty. We will also borrow energy to run our machine-making factory. As the factory is fully automated, it does not need people to operate it".

"Maybe we should make two factories and give

one back to Morty. What do you think?" asked Chen.

The group agreed.

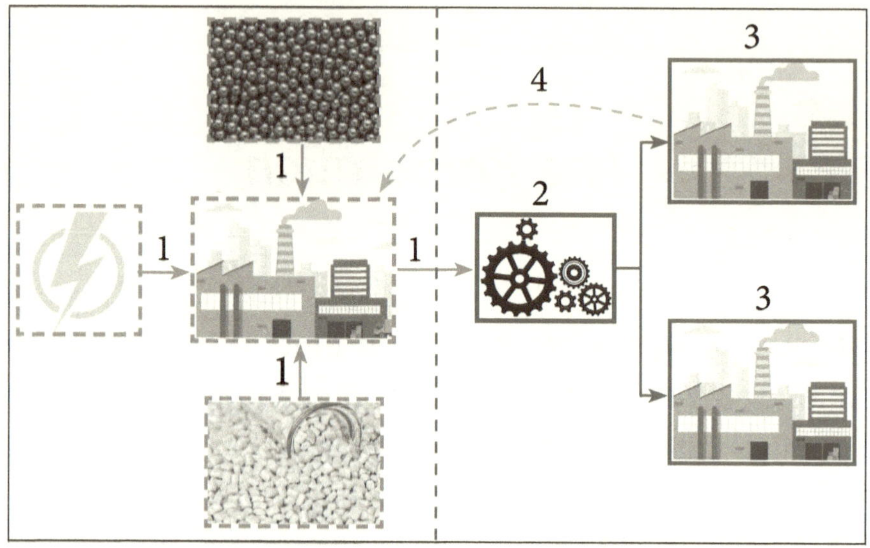

1- Borrow Factory, Raw Materials [Metal, Plastic] and power to run the Factory.
2- Make machines from borrowed factory.
3- With the machines make two "machine-making factories" same as the one you borrowed.
4- Return one factory to Morty. Keep one to make other machines.

"How does the visual look?" asked Chen.

"What is that blue dotted line?" asked Emma.

"Oh. Everything on the left of the line is borrowed stuff and the numbers relate to my description of the process in the visual", said Chen.

"Looks alright. I think this will help", said Meg.

"By the way, what do you think we should call our machine-making factory?" asked Emma.

There was animated discussion around the room

with various options being proposed. Emma noted them down on pieces of paper, crumpled them and dropped them on the table. Chen picked on and opened it for others to see. The paper had the word Shuru on it.

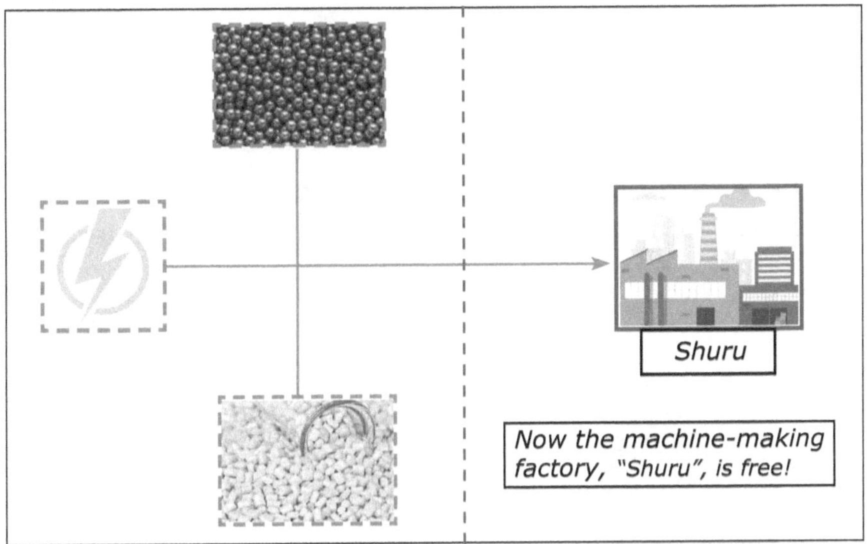

"What does that mean?" asked Chen to the group not knowing who had written it. Karan replied, "It means the beginning". The group agreed that the name made sense and decided to name their machine-making factory Shuru.

Meg continued, "The first machines Shuru will make are machines needed to build a power plant. We will build a fully automated power plant that will start producing electricity".

"What kind of power plant?" asked Karan. "I would prefer to generate clean power and would propose we go solar. Shuru can make all the solar panels and construction robots needed for building the solar power plants".

The group agreed to build solar power plants to generate clean electricity.

Meg said, "From now on, we do not need to take Morty's free energy anymore. We could even return all the energy that we have borrowed till now".

There were smiles around the room with kin saying, "Take that, Morty". The group burst out into

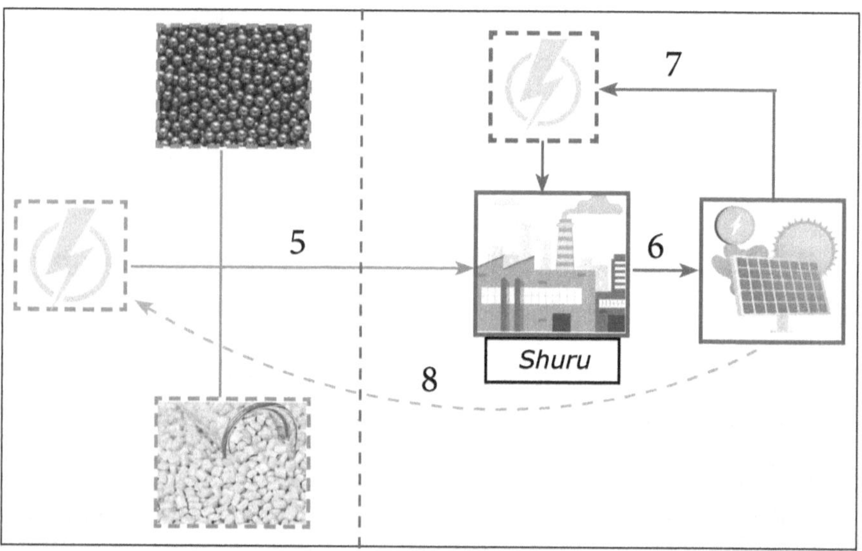

5- Borrow Raw Materials [Metal, Plastic] and power to run our Factory - Shuru.
6- Make power plants - Solar.
7- Start running Shuru with your power [electricity]
8- Return all borrowed power back to Morty.

laughter as Morty's last minute change had caused a fair amount of grief in the group.

"Next, we get Shuru to make all machines needed to build a fully automated hydrogen plant. Hydrogen will be our clean portable energy option and will replace hydrocarbons like petrol, diesel, aviation fuel, etc.

So, now we will have free energy, both wired and portable for all of our activities", Meg concluded. The group showed their appreciation clapping loudly.

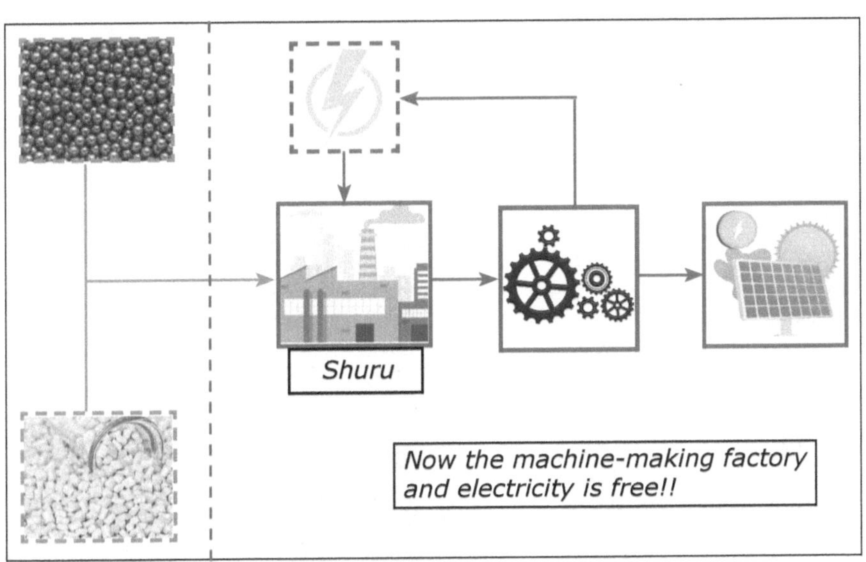

Karan said, "We then get back to our earlier plan. We get Shuru to make fully automated mining and mineral processing machines and factories. With our free energy, now metal will be free. And we return all the metal that we have borrowed till now".

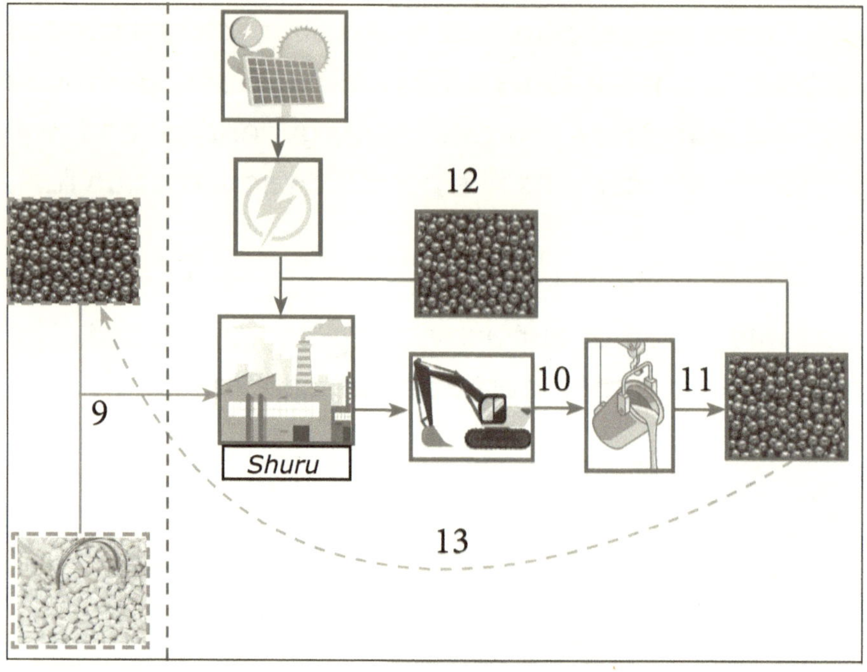

9- Borrow Raw Materials [Metal, Plastic] to run our Factory - Shuru.
10- Make mining machines and mineral processing machines.
11- Make Metal.
12- Use your Metal as raw material for Shuru.
13- Return all borrowed metal back to Morty.

Meg added, "We can take the same approach with plastics as well. We get Shuru to make fully automated drilling, refining and plastic-making machines and factories. With our free energy, now plastic will be free, and we return all the plastic that we have borrowed till now to Morty".

Chen asked, "What is the point in giving Morty the raw materials back? From this point onwards, it is all

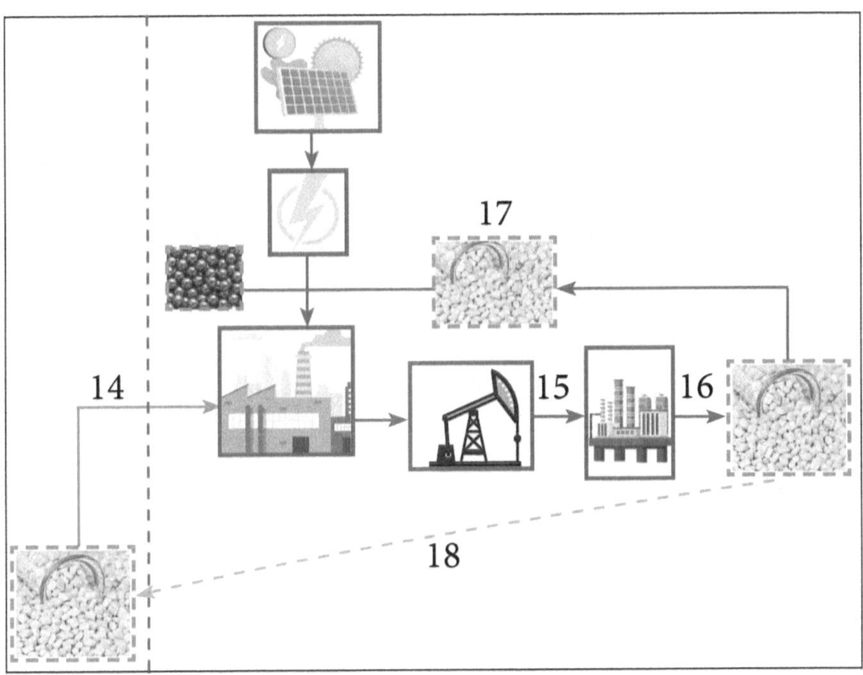

14- Borrow Raw Material [Plastic] to run Shuru.
15- Make Oil drill, Refinery and Petro chemical factories.
16- Make Plastic.
17- Use Plastic as raw material for Shuru.
18- Return all borrowed Plastic back to Morty.

free for everyone. Isn't it?"

Emma said, "And why give Morty the power back as that is going to be free as well".

The group pondered over this for a while mildly puzzled. Why did Morty want it back?

Miya suggested that they flag this to Morty and if he still wanted all his raw material, machines and power back, he was free to take it.

Miya said, "This is where we really break free. No more borrowing of energy or raw materials. We have started to make everything on our own. From now on, we can make whatever we want for free".

"The blue dotted line is gone", said Chen. The group cheered.

Miya continued, "We get Shuru to make machines to build a fully automated desalination plant and pump stations to pump the water wherever we want. With free machines, free energy and no people, fresh water is now free.

We then get Shuru to make machines to build a fully automated fertilizer factory. With free machines, free energy, free hydrocarbons and no people, the fertilizer we make is free".

Chen added, "Shuru then makes all machines needed to plant, maintain and harvest the crops. The machines will be free and will be powered by free energy. With free irrigated water, free fertilizer and free farming machines, we can grow grass and feed for cows and sugar cane for sugar".

Miya continued, "Now we will get Shuru to make all machines required to milk and take care of the cows. We will build a fully automated dairy farm where drones herd and manage the cows, milking machines to milk the cows and churning machines to make cream.

Shuru will also make machines to transport the milk and cream to the ice cream factory".

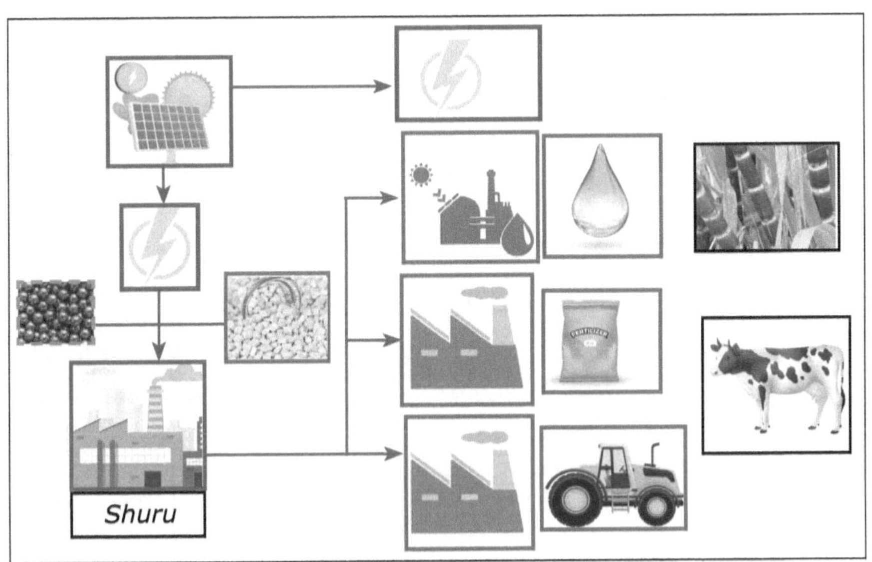

Power Plant = free electricity
Desalination plant = free water
Fertiliser factory = free fertiliser
Free Electricity + Water + Fertilizer + Farm machines
= Free farm produce for all

Karan joined in and said, "Shuru will make machines to build a fully automated Sugar Mill. Our free farming equipment will harvest the cane, our free transport equipment will take it to the Sugar Mill and the mill will extract the sugarcane juice, heat it up with free energy and make free sugar".

Emma stood up and said, "Well, we are on the home stretch now. Shuru will make all machines needed for us to build a fully automated ice cream factory. With free energy, free machines, free water and free raw materials like milk, cream and sugar, we

can make free ice cream for everyone forever".
The group cheered in unison.

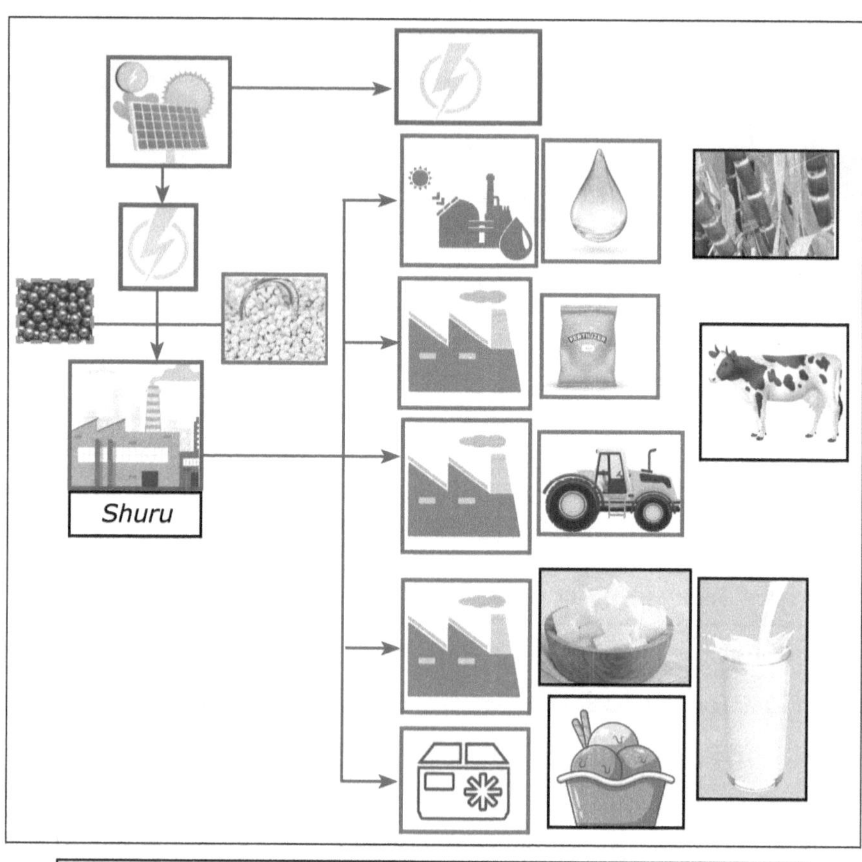

Power Plant = free electricity
Desalination plant = free water
Fertiliser factory = free fertiliser
Free Electricity + Water + Fertilizer + Farm machines
= Free farm produce for all

Free Electricity + Raw materials + Machines/Factories
= Free Ice Cream for all

Miya said, "OK guys. That is excellent. Now can we all pull all the supporting material and pictures and compile this presentation".

Free Everything

The next day while the group was compiling the presentation, Meg said, "I was thinking about something that Emma said the other day. Do you remember when she said, 'if you can raise free sugar cane why not free grass or other cattle feed?'"

"What about it?" asked Karan.

"Well, if you can raise free sugar cane why not free Wheat or Rice or Corn or Maize?" asked Meg.

"That is a good point. But what has that to do with making free ice cream?" asked Karan looking at Meg with an amused look.

Meg got flustered with his response and said, "We could eliminate global poverty, you idiot".

Karan smiled and said, "Hey cool. I knew exactly where you were coming from. Just wanted to rile you up".

"So, all grown food can be absolutely free?" asked Emma shaking her head.

"And you were the one who planted this seed", said Meg.

"Even fruits and vegetables", said Karan and continued, "If you have software to recognize faces why can't we have drones picking the fruit or vegetable at the right condition?"

Miya said, "If we take the same approach, we already have a cost-free dairy farm to produce milk. We can also create cost-free cattle, sheep and poultry farms to produce meat".

"So, all food can be absolutely free", said Chen and continued, "Even processed food, as they will all be made in food factories similar to our free ice cream factory".

"I was thinking of something similar but didn't want to take the focus away from the project", said Karan, "and it goes like this. I know something about cars. So, let us consider a car. I think a car is made up of many components and most of the components are made of either metal or plastic. If so, based on our model, a car could be manufactured for free. And with free fuel, say hydrogen, every person could have a free car".

"OMG, if a car can be made free, what else!" exclaimed Chen.

"Look, there is a lot of things out there and we can spend years checking up on each and everything to see if it can be made free. Question is, do we have the time, keeping in mind this presentation is due in two days' time", responded Miya.

"I agree. We have been given a specific assignment – to make free ice cream. We now have the solution. I think we should present this, get our grades, which I believe will be fairly good, and move on. I don't want to be stuck in this project for the rest of my life", said Karan.

"I think it is a valid point", said Meg. "However, we have opened an interesting option that probably needs to be explored. So, here is my suggestion. You guys complete the presentation while Chen and I follow this idea through".

The group agreed.

Meg and Chen decided to explore the new option and moved to the next room to continue the discussion while the rest of the group continued to put together the presentation.

Once they were in the adjacent room, Chen said, "Where do we start?"

"Let us try to understand what is it that we really want to do here?" said Meg. "Are we going to list each and everything made by humans and then see if that thing can be made free? There could be a million things ... pen, paper, pencil ...", said Meg.

"Ships, Trains, Airplanes, Buses ...", added Chen.

"TVs, Phones, Computers ...", continued Meg.

"Shoes, Pants, Shirts ...", said Chen and continued, "OK, we cannot list everything. It is impossible", he concluded.

"But it is such an intriguing idea, isn't it?" asked Meg, "Everything for free, not just ice cream. I think it is worth talking to someone. Morty is not in for the next couple of days. I guess that leaves us with the hill", said Meg.

"Let us do it", said Chen and off they went to catch a bus.

Up at the hill, Prof. Iyer gave them a bright smile when they tabled this idea of free everything.

"Yes. In a nutshell, anything that is manufactured or grown is a prime candidate to be made free of cost.

Let us take a shirt as an example. The fabric may be cotton or wool. Wool comes from the farm, same as cotton. They are in turn taken through many machines till it is converted to fabric. With automated shirt-making machines, all shirts can be made free.

A TV or a computer is a metal or plastic outer with printed circuit boards and other electronic components inside, all of which are a combination of metal and other man-made materials like plastics and glass. So, effectively, these items can be made free.

Keep in mind that the hardware becomes free, not the software, which is the creative content. But that will also become free over a period of time based on the patent or Intellectual Property laws".

Prof. Iyer took a deep breath and said, "Your idea is going to create a massive disruption to the world economy. Each and every industry sector and business out there will have to figure out how this idea will impact them and how they are going to transition through this change. Not-for-profit outfits will move into this space progressively as the idea picks up pace.

In the new world, the only thing that will cost you is new ideas and creative concepts that deliver real value for people.

If you were to introduce a new flavour of ice cream to the market and if people love it, you can charge people for the same. But keep in mind that your cost of manufacturing the new flavour ice cream will still be zero. So, in effect, you will only be charging people for your new idea.

Further, a new poem or piece of literature, a new musical performance, and any new artistic endeavour may not be free as long as people value it. Keep in mind that the delivery mechanism, like a book or device, by itself will be free, but not the creative content".

"I can tell you this much for free", the Prof. smiled at the poor pun and continued, "Thanks to you kids, it is going to be a very different world out there".

CHAPTER 18

The Presentation

There were two people at the podium with Morty. Morty introduced them to the class as senior advisors from the state educational board. They had been invited by Morty to observe this presentation. The man had chubby cheeks and had the look of an overgrown baby. The lady had her hair pulled back in a bun and looked stern.

Morty kicked off the session by providing an overview of what was the scope of the project provided to the group and what were the constraints and limitations.

Morty then spelled out the process for the presentation session. The group would have forty-five minutes to present. The rest of the class would have fifteen minutes to think about the presentation and come up with queries and comments on the presentation.

The group would have to address the critique

and defend their presentation. If they were unable to present a response to the queries posed, they could request for time, do further research and get back to the class with suitable responses by next week.

The class agreed to these ground rules.

The group started their presentation. They opened with Morty's brief and went through the rest of the presentation as they had prepared and rehearsed the previous day.

The group had also added a final "by the way" slide to indicate that their solution would not only make ice cream free but would also make all food and manufactured items free.

At the end of the presentation, the silence was rocking.

The rest of the class was in shock at the concept and the solution the group had proposed. Slowly, the class started discussing the presentation and the murmur level in the class gradually rose.

The group could see Morty in serious conversation with the advisors. When Morty ambled across to them, they could see him smiling. Morty looked mighty pleased.

Morty said, "You guys just hit it out of the ballpark. Amazing show. That free-everything was a real blinder". He continued sheepishly, "And I must apologize for asking for my machines and raw materials back. I really didn't think that through, did I?"

When the fifteen minutes were up, Morty turned to the class and said, "Comments and critique please".

The first comment came from the Green corner. "You guys talk about mining minerals and using them to make machines and other things. Minerals are finite resources. Will we not run out of them?"

The group huddled to discuss. Chen said he would wing it and address this question. Chen stood up and said, "A big part of our strategy will be to recycle. All old machines that get replaced will be stripped apart by robots and all metal will be recycled".

There were warm taps on Chen's shoulders as he sat down.

The Green corner came back again. "We understand that your project is going to deliver large amounts of plastics as part of everything that is made. Plastics are not biodegradable and are notoriously difficult to recycle. We are currently struggling to manage plastic waste. Our oceans and waterways are getting littered with plastics. Will your project not make this worse?"

Miya winced. She had been bothered with this issue right from the start.

The group went into a huddle, had a quick chat and asked for time to respond to this criticism. Morty agreed and asked them for the response by next Wednesday.

The Yellow corner put their hand up and said, "Your project proposes having fully automated factories producing things that people want. How will this work? And where is the incentive for someone to make a better product. Will this mean that what we get today will be the same thing that we will get forever?"

"That is a brilliant question", Morty commented and turned around to the group for a response. The group waved back indicating they will respond on Wednesday.

"Any further comments or criticism?" Morty asked. The class seemed to be quiet. As Morty was about to wrap up the session, he saw Emma walking away from the group.

There were puzzled looks around as Emma went to the other side of the class, turned around and said, "I have one".

The group was in shock.

Morty said, "Go on".

Emma said, "The project is built on the basis that all factories will be fully automated, and no people will be required to operate them. If we do this, what will all the people do for jobs?"

The group was frozen for a while. Presently Chen waved back to Morty indicating they would field this critique on Wednesday as well.

As the class started to break up, Meg could see Morty talking to the two advisors. She could hear the advisors saying that the presentation was brilliant and that they should take it further. Meg wondered, "further where?"

The group members gathered outside the class and started discussing the presentation. Miya said, "Guys, it would be better if went over to the Project Room for our discussion". As the group started to move towards the project room, Miya realized Emma was not with them. She looked back to find Emma and the advisor having an animated conversation at the far end of the room.

The group members convened at the Project Room. Emma was not there. The mood was mixed with some joy about the successful presentation, some concern about the critique and how they were going to address it. But the predominant feeling in the group was the taste of betrayal. The dominant opinion was that Emma had knifed them in the back. "But why do this at the presentation" was the question running through everyone's mind.

Miya waved her hands to get everyone's attention and said, "I think it went well". There was a general murmur of consent. Miya continued, "Let us divvy up the critique and nominate who wants to address what".

The innovation aspect was something they had not considered. Meg said she will give it a shot. Miya offered to work with Meg on this critique. The group was sure that this aspect needed some hard work.

"I know I raised this issue of drowning in plastic. To be fair, I could not come up with an alternate solution given our project limitations. However, it looks like we are cornered, and we need to respond now", said Miya.

Chen and Karan seemed to think they could do some research and find a suitable response to the issue of plastics.

'So, we do something only when we are cornered; no wonder Emma went over', thought Miya.

And then there was the elephant in the room that they had to address. But seriously, no one wanted to as it made them very emotional.

Miya said, "Look, do you think we are also at fault with this Emma situation?"

The response was a bit rough and ranged from "WHAT?" to "are you out of your mind?"

Miya continued, "To be fair, Emma had always raised this issue. We had our blinkers on and were just focused on getting to what we thought was a workable solution. Unfortunately, she doesn't think it is a good workable solution".

Meg said, "Look guys, I understand where she is

coming from. It is very personal to her. I think she and her family had a rough time when her dad was between jobs and had to retrain to land a new job".

Meg continued, "We didn't want to address the issue then. But now that she has brought it out, we are forced to deal with it".

Karan was bitter. "This will take us right back to square one", he said. "If we take out the automation option, the whole aspect of people cost will come back and our solution will not work".

Miya said, "Leave it with me. I have some ideas on this front. But do we all agree that we did not really address her concerns and sidelined her?"

There was as a gentle murmur indicating a half-hearted agreement.

"Ok, let us proceed on that basis", concluded Miya.

They all agreed to meet again in three days. That would give them sufficient time to address the critique and develop a good response.

CHAPTER 19

The Defence

Three days later, the group convened in the Project Room. Everyone was surprised to see Emma in attendance as well.

On plastics, Karan and Chen had done some research online to get an understanding of the issues with recycling plastics. There was a wealth of information available and it took them a while to sift through and make notes. Subsequently, they had also visited the local waste management centre to get a better understanding of the issue and potential solution.

Karan kicked off by saying, "Yes, there is a solution to the plastic waste issue. It is recycling. The problem is, there are different types of plastics and they will not mix. For plastic recycling to work, we need to segregate plastic material based on its type. We must be able to effectively collect and sort plastic. That is the key. The funny thing is, once we have done that, we have the technology to recycle most kinds of plastic".

Chen said, "So, our solution is that every plastic item that is manufactured will have a visual code, that people can see and sort, and will also have a micro tag that automated sorters can recognize and send it to the right bin for it to be recycled. It is a big job, given that our current waste management is fairly primitive, but we have the technology to make it happen".

On the issues of sustaining innovation, Meg and Miya had done some work and were keen to share it with the group. Meg said, "Look, both of us had a discussion on this and have formed a view. Let us know what you think. Okay?"

Meg continued, "Some questions to address. How will this Model work?"

Miya answered, "The people who want to make a new ice cream decide on the recipe, list the raw materials needed and the details of how the ice cream is to be made. They feed this information into the ice cream manufacturing pod. It sources the free raw material and makes the ice cream".

"What if the new ice cream is of poor quality and makes people sick", asked Chen.

"As a minimum, all current regulations and approval processes will apply to all things made in the new world", said Miya.

Meg continued, "Next question. Why will someone do all this work for free?"

Miya answered, "Charities and non-profit organizations work for free. At the individual level, volunteers and Pro Bono professionals seem to be doing a lot of free work as well. Not everyone is only motivated by money. For some, it may be because they already have enough and want to give something back. For others, it may be other forms of gratification like accolades or Peer or Social recognition that motivates them".

Meg commented, "Keep in mind that with everything free, you might not really need the money. Money may not be the biggest motivator in the new world".

Meg continued, "Next question. Why will someone want to create something new? What is the incentive for new ideas?"

Miya answered, "For pretty much the same reasons as earlier. For instance, let us say Miya introduces a new flavour of ice cream to the market and names it 'Miyazz'. The ice cream is a hit; people love it. Social media is abuzz with Miya being the creator of the new ice cream. Miya becomes famous. Now, Miya can either charge people for the ice cream and make money or she can keep it free and enjoy the social gratification or do both".

Meg continued, "Once you have a new idea, it is much easier to implement it. Could be the next gen TV or footwear or whatever. Your job as the creator is to design the new product. You tell the manufacturing pod what raw materials are needed and how they should be processed to create your version of the product.

The manufacturing pod will get the raw materials and make your product for free. There is no cost. You can charge a nominal amount that you think your new idea deserves. If people love it and think it is special, they will pay for it".

"Keep in mind that new ideas have a time limitation based on the agreed Intellectual Property or Patent laws", Miya gently reminded the group.

"Does that address the issue of innovation?" asked Meg.

The group agreed that it did.

"OK, so that leaves us with the issue of People. Who is going to address this?" asked Miya.

There was silence around the room till Emma gently stepped up and said, "I have got that covered".

CHAPTER 20

The Change

"Is your surname Hegel?" asked Chen. The rest of the group stared at Chen with a confused look.

Emma smiled and said, "Not really. I did not create this issue to drive a solution. I was keenly aware that this is a big issue that needed to be addressed. But unfortunately, the group did not share my concerns. So, I tabled it at the presentation".

Emma continued, "I have been doing some work on this in the background. I have had long chats with the professor of sociology at our local college about this. She helped me a lot in getting clarity on how to address this issue. So, here is the solution".

The group was all ears.

"The first thing is accepting the fact that automation is in".

Emma could see Karan breathing a sigh of relief as she continued, "It is not going to go away. It is already happening to some extent in some parts of the world. It does lead to job losses and has a massive impact on people.

We are already seeing effects of job losses whether it is due to automation or factories going offshore for cheaper labour. We are seeing a marked rise in 'nationalism' among various countries. People wanting to close borders, isolate themselves and trying to go back to the 'good-old-days' hoping to get the lost jobs back.

Interestingly, we are trying to accelerate this process with our project. This will be a major change event and made worse because it happens fast. This will create a massive upheaval globally, for sure.

If people cannot put food on the table for their families, they will revolt. We have all done the major revolutions in our history class and have learned from it. Do you agree?"

There was general agreement among the group.

"So, the question is how to avert this disaster?" asked Emma and continued, "One major advantage with our solution is that it is structured in a progressive manner. We have a sequential order where industries get transformed and become cost free.

As per our model, first it will be the power generation industry that will be totally automated, then mining and mineral processing, petrochemicals and so on. So, not all industries will become people free at the same time. It will happen progressively. Let us assume it takes twenty years for each industry to go free.

We need a plan for people who are already working in the industry. The people who are currently close to retirement will probably not be affected by this change. But the younger workers who have just joined the industry will need a plan".

"I think one of the most important things we need to do is to tell people that these changes are coming up in the next twenty years and plans have been put in place for a smooth transition".

Emma continued, "Based on our assumption, a twenty-year-old who has just joined the industry will be forty years old when these changes come into play. That person will probably have a family and kids to support. So, I think we should have a retraining programme for all of those people.

We need to have a programme where all of the younger workers could go back to school and get trained in the new skills they will be needing in twenty years' time. That way, when the industry shifts to automation, most of these people will have the necessary skills to make a smooth transition.

Under our project model, areas like AI and Automation will have a very high demand for people in the coming decades".

"Impressive, but how will this work? Who will pay for all this retraining?" Karan peppered Emma with questions.

Emma took a deep breath and said, "I believe that we the people need to pay for this. By that, I mean, the government pays for this from our tax dollars. We could design it where each person gets reimbursed for any course that they take and can even be rewarded for successfully completing the course. It will not be a handout because we the people fund the cost of the course while the person invests their time and effort in learning a new skill. I think it is a win-win approach".

"Good point", said Meg, "I also think that it will be much cheaper to invest in people now than to try and contain a full-blown revolt later".

Emma continued, "I did look at the educational system in a couple of countries. The Indian system of heavily subsidized technology education in colleges seems to have done well. Over the past few decades, India has generated many engineers who have helped with the country taking a significant role in the IT sector. That investment by the Indian government seems to have paid off.

The Australian model seems interesting too. I think they have interest-free student loans that only need to be repaid when the person starts to earn above a certain salary and even then, they only pay a small portion of their salary every month as loan repayment. So, it almost feels like the education is free".

"What happens to those who do not have a flair for the new technology? What happens to those who will not be interested in learning the new technology?" asked Karan.

"I have given it a thought as well", said Emma. "Not everyone needs to become an automation expert. While most of the factories will become automated, there will still be some that might shift to making boutique products that will still require labour and there will be jobs for those people", said Emma.

"Looks like it comes down to understanding where the demand will be and help people to educate, train and skill themselves up for the new demand", said Chen.

"And we need to communicate this clearly to people. If they know that there is a way out of this maze, they will not panic and will work towards the solution", said Meg.

Emma said, "I also realized that this issue of job losses is only during the transition. As per our model, once the automation is bedded in, all food and manufactured goods will be free for all people. From that point onwards, people do not have to work to earn a living. Instead people can learn and work in those areas that they love – work for their passion".

"That sounds really beautiful", said Miya. "All of your basic requirements are met, and you are free to do whatever is your passion. Just loving that thought".

Emma said, "There is one another key issue. Any social solution on such a scale will require political support. While the change we are proposing will take decades to implement, our political systems run on a short cycle with governments up for the next election every three to five years. This programme can become a political hot potato during elections and get derailed".

"So, here is the solution. We should have an independent body, say a Change Board, similar to central Banks, to manage this change. The Board will be funded, have a clear charter and guidelines and will be almost independent of the elected government. Governments may come and go but the Board soldiers on to make this change happen".

The group agreed that this was a good plan to address what was till then the elephant in the room.

CHAPTER 21

To the Town Hall

The group convened in the Project Room when Morty hurried in. He seemed to be slightly flustered and said, "Do we have the defence ready?"

Miya stepped forward and confirmed that they were.

"All of it?" asked Morty. "The issue with plastics, the issue with innovation and the issue with loss of jobs. All of it?"

The group said in unison, "Yes, Mr. Morty".

"Well, I'll be ...", Morty trailed off and said, "OK let us hear it".

"Weren't we supposed to do it in the classroom?" queried Miya.

"Yes, but slight change of plans. This project has generated a lot of interest in the stratosphere". Morty had his hands pointing upwards, "The district board, our local political representatives, some media, you name it, they all want to know about this project.

Therefore, we have organized for a presentation for this evening at the Town Hall. We have sent invites to all of your parents and all the other people whom you have been talking to and getting guidance from, as well. It is going to be a big crowd this evening and we might end up in the news as well".

The group was in mild shock.

"My preference was to go ahead with the presentation you made in class and leave out the critique. Now you tell me that you have addressed it already. Let's hear it".

Karan and Chen came forward and provided a brief summary of their proposed solution to managing plastics. Morty took it in and nodded saying, "OK we can add that to the end of the presentation as response to the critique".

Meg and Miya came forward and proposed their theory on how the model will work and how innovation will not be stymied. Morty gave a thumbs-up and looked around to Emma.

Emma provided her summary of the proposed solution to large-scale job losses and managing the change. Morty smiled at Emma not saying anything. Emma responded with a smile acknowledging what was not being said.

"OK guys. Let us all be at the Town Hall. 6:30 for 7:00. Smart casual dress code. I do not expect any critique to be coming up in this session. If it does, I will take it offline and keep the evening going. By the way, do you guys think that this whole solution will actually work?" asked Morty.

"Of course, Mr. Morty. We are absolutely sure", the group responded in unison.

"In that case, after you complete your presentation, you need to ask the media and others to take this concept out there to the rest of the world. You need to ask the political representatives to take this concept forward and initiate action".

"It is time to make this happen", said Morty.

BOOK 2

MAKE IT HAPPEN

CHAPTER 1

Meg

As Meg started walking towards the building, she realized that she still hadn't gotten used to the funny glass pyramid–like structure in front of the building. It was not imposing, not artistic and certainly did not go with the building, which was no great shakes to start with.

As she got on the first step, her phone chimed. "More congratulations, I suppose", she thought with a wry smile. With social media the way it was, any "special" day just went crazy. "All people had to do was to press a button to send a caring preset message", Meg thought. And it looked like people took this social duty pretty seriously.

Meg had been working for the last few years at the Department of Foreign Affairs in Canberra, Australia. She had already gotten her message that morning from Emma who was based in Los Angeles. Looked like Emma was one of the few who abstained from clicking on preset messages.

Emma's parents had separated and she, with her mother, had moved over to the States right after school. She had family in the west coast of the United States and had settled down in California. She had joined the local university, after school, to pursue higher studies in the study of History and Human Resources. People and their issues remained her fascination.

Meg recalled her last conversation with Emma. Emma had joined one of the NGOs in the region and was waxing lyrical about the diverse groups and views and how she was engaging and interacting with them to bring together a cohesive approach with a common central theme.

Making her way up in the lift, Meg reflected on her time at the service.

She enjoyed her work, most of the time. It was always different. One day she was researching and digging up details on the artichoke trade with Andorra and the other day she was collating data on a division of the Chinese army placed in the outer reaches of Mongolia. She rarely got an insight into where that information was being used or its importance in the scheme of things.

But it was clear that it was very important; it was always needed by yesterday.

Getting to her desk and logging in, Meg took a quick look at her in tray and confirmed that none of those explosive requests had landed on her desk, yet. 'Give it time', she thought.

Opening her calendar, Meg realized that she had a one-on-one with Palucci. When she joined the service, Meg had signed up for a myriad of development programmes that the service offered. While at times painful, it certainly helped her cohort to socialize and develop professional relationships with senior bureaucrats. Palucci was one of her mentors in one of those programmes. Meg set aside some time in the morning to do some prep work for the lunch session with Palucci.

Her phone chimed again. It was Miya, mindlessly clicking a preset "Congrats" message. Meg had been keeping in touch with Miya. To be fair, it was Miya who kept in touch with Meg, calling and talking with Meg on a regular basis.

Both Meg and Miya had joined the university in Canberra after school. Both had pursued their interest in Global Studies, International Relations and Economics. In their final year at the University, Miya had decided that she was going over to her ancestral home, India, to implement the FrICE solution there.

Meg was not sure if that was the right move. "I wouldn't suggest it. Just because you look Indian, and you have an Indian heritage, it doesn't mean you are one. Believe me, you are a local. Your cultural roots may be there, in part, but you were born and raised here. It is a very different place to what we are used to. You will struggle over there, and I have a bad feeling about this".

Miya had still gone over to India. The first few weeks were a disaster. There were times when Miya was in tears and very close to coming back home. Miya would call Meg on a weekly basis and the two would chat about her experiences in India. Meg suggested that having gone all the way, Miya might as well tough it out for a while and then decide to pack her bags if things still did not work out.

In the first month, Miya had landed a job with a global consultancy firm and had been assigned to work in the energy sector on renewable energy projects. Miya was thrilled that things were going in the right direction on the work front. However, she was still battling the myriad of cultural variances that really made life very interesting, for want of a better term.

Things picked up from then on and Miya was reasonably settled in her job. She slowly found herself adapting to life in India. Miya and Meg continued to keep in touch regularly. A few weeks back, their conversation had turned to the Free Ice Cream Project.

"You know what, it has been years since we did Morty's project. Do you know if anyone in our project group has started to do anything in that direction?" Miya had asked. Meg had replied in the negative and said, "It bothers me too, from time to time. Here was this amazing global solution that we had proposed and no further action? I do not think it is right. If we do not push it, who else will?" Ironically, both had agreed on that comment and had moved on to other things to discuss.

Meg's calendar popped up reminding her to prep up for the meeting with Palucci. Meg pulled herself to the task in hand. As she started to make notes, she stopped. Meg started thinking, why can't I talk about the free ice cream concept with Palucci. He is fairly senior in the organization. He has access to the cabinet. And he has years of experience in dealing with this bureaucracy.

She mulled it over for a while and decided. "And that is exactly what I am going to do", Meg mumbled to herself forcefully and started searching for the Free Ice Cream Project summary she drew up a few years back. She quickly went over the material and got ready to go to the cafeteria to meet with Palucci.

Coffee was on her.

CHAPTER 2

Coffee with Palucci

The cafeteria was fairly deserted. Meg selected a cubicle with a view to the entrance waiting for Palucci. Palucci was of average height, balding and looked middle aged as he entered the cafeteria. He was sporting a jacket with no tie, a semi-casual look. Meg waved and Palucci spotted her.

"How is it going?" Palucci asked, once seated.

"It is going good", replied Meg and continued, "But there is one specific topic that I wanted to discuss with you today".

"Shoot", said Palucci.

"A few years back, when I was in high school, we did a project. The assignment was to figure out how to give ice cream free, to everyone, forever. We found a solution, a way to manufacture and give ice cream free to everyone forever".

Meg could see Palucci's brows knotting up. Meg continued, "And through that process, we also found a way to make everything free for everyone forever".

Palucci had raised his hand and said, "You were one of the kids in that project?" Meg nodded. "Well, that was a few years back, right?" Palucci continued without expecting the answer, "You guys were impressive. What I remember the most is the silence from the economists". Palucci was smiling big and said, "You guys did good".

"Thank you", said Meg and continued, "How much of our model do you still remember?"

"Wouldn't mind a refresh on the overview", Palucci replied.

Meg gave him a brief of the solution – free automated machines built with free metals and plastic and running on free energy to manufacture everything free for everyone.

Meg said, "I want to have a chat with you to figure out how to make that concept happen".

Palucci's smile froze.

"You want to make the concept happen", Palucci repeated.

Seeing Palucci's response, Meg thought for a moment and then said, "Can we at least have a chat about the first step of the process?"

"And what would that be?" asked Palucci.

"Free clean energy for everyone", said Meg.

Palucci drew a long breath, pondered for a while

and said, "Let us consider just one part of your statement. Drop the 'free' and let us just focus on clean energy for everyone. In the current environment, I believe that is where things are going, at least here in Australia. It is highly unlikely that new coal-based power stations are going to be approved".

Palucci continued, "The current social and political climate is against coal. Regulations do not favour it. Even commercially, renewables seem to be making better sense. The finance sector has pretty much stopped looking at any proposal based on coal. The insurance sector will not touch it with a barge pole. In this environment, the renewables win hands down, don't they?" asked Palucci.

"True", said Meg, "but organic growth of clean renewable energy alone will not suffice. We need to make it free as well".

"And how would you achieve that?" asked Palucci.

"Free energy is the first piece in the 'Free Economy' solution. With free energy, we can make free machines and subsequently free everything for everyone. As the first step, the 'free energy' solution should be commercially viable and self-sustaining over the long term. It will be fine for the government to prop up the programme for a short while, but we want it to be self-sustaining in the long run".

"The clean energy model that we talked about is

certainly commercially viable and self-sustaining. It is market driven", commented Palucci.

"Not when the energy is going to be given away for free", replied Meg.

Palucci hummed.

"We need a commercially viable model that will enable recovery of investment and generation of profits for the investors while also enabling delivery of free energy", said Meg.

"Wow. That is a very interesting requirement. How are we going to do that?" asked Palucci.

"I have some ideas. I have put together a model that indicates that it can be done. But that model is something I would want you to review, try to take it apart".

"I would love to take a look at the model", said Palucci.

"Thank you", said Meg and continued, "so, that is the first requirement. Next, we need to build our renewable energy capacity to many times of our current energy needs".

Palucci raised his eyebrows questioning this statement.

"Some of the additional energy that we produce is going to be used to generate hydrogen. We are going to be supplying the world with portable hydrogen power.

In the initial phase, we can sell some of this hydrogen in the global market for a price. That revenue will be one of the factors that will assist with making the Free Energy Programme commercially viable and self-sustaining over the long term", said Meg.

"If it is a Free Energy Programme, how come you are selling the hydrogen?" questioned Palucci.

"The idea is to facilitate a gradual transition. When we start the programme, the plan is to sell part of our production and feed the remaining energy to the Free Energy Programme. We gradually ramp up free energy to a hundred percent. We are not going to flick a switch and jump into a free economy", said Meg.

"So, it looks like the energy sales will continue till we recover our investment in the renewable energy infrastructure", said Palucci.

"In principle, yes. We can go through the details when we review the Free Energy Model", said Meg.

"This is getting interesting. Any other requirements?" said Palucci.

"Sure. Some of the additional energy that we produce is going to be used to make water. With desalination, we are not a desert anymore. We can be the food basket of the world".

"Interesting", said Palucci.

"And that could be another source of income

from the other countries. Similar to what we do with energy, we can initially sell some of the food that we produce and provide the rest for free and gradually ramp up free food to a hundred percent", said Meg.

Meg continued, "The next requirement is that some of the additional energy is going to be used to extract the carbon dioxide from the atmosphere and bury it back where it came from; sequester it in the old depleted oil wells".

"Why would we want to do that?" asked Palucci.

"Because it has to be done; all the carbon dioxide that we have pumped into the atmosphere over the decades and centuries has to be pulled back; the damage has to be repaired. Carbon Capture and Storage is not new. It is a tried and tested technology.

This can certainly be used as a business model. Over the coming decades, I believe that the clean-up will become a responsibility of all the past and present polluters – the big corporations and industrialized nations. We demonstrate to the world that we can repair the damage in a cost-effective manner.

Other countries can do it themselves or we can do it for them as a paid service during the development of the Free Economy model and gradually ramp it down to a free service. The beauty is that this is a service that transcends borders and we can deliver it from our backyard.

As you can see, with this requirement for abundant energy, all the three focus areas, i.e., global source of hydrogen, food and carbon dioxide clean-up service, will serve as a good commercial model for us to ramp up the Free Energy Programme and ultimately the Free Economy Programme", said Meg.

"And you have not considered organic solutions like afforestation or soil capture, to extract the carbon dioxide, have you", asked Palucci and seeing Meg's silence said, "Okay, what is next", asked Palucci.

Meg said, "The next important requirement is that this transition needs to be fast tracked. We need to move to complete clean power and hit the other targets at the earliest".

Palucci's knotted eyebrows expressed his confusion.

Meg said, "I think the countries that get there first, the countries that generate surplus clean renewable energy, will have a dominant role in global economy. It is possible for these dominant countries to set the agenda to take us all to a free economy".

"Okay. What is the next issue?" asked Palucci.

"Next issue is one of the critical ones", Meg continued, "With big changes like these, I don't think it would be reasonable to expect success if people are not behind it. And if people support it, the governments and politicians will be very supportive. Right?"

"Doesn't happen every time, but in principle I agree", said Palucci.

Meg continued, "For this transition to be successful, we should have a clear plan with relief structures for those people who would be impacted by these decisions – people working in or benefitting from the traditional power sector.

The political leadership should take this concept and sell it to their people. The governments should clearly explain how people will benefit from this change. More importantly, leaders need to explain how their people will NOT be negatively impacted by this transition to clean energy decisions.

"Any more requirements?" asked Palucci.

Meg sensed that something was off; Palucci's tone was off and so was the facial expression.

Without waiting for Meg's answer, Palucci continued, "Look you are a bright, young, upcoming member of our services team. That is one of the reasons I accepted to be your mentor in this development programme.

Frankly, I was hoping to come to lunch at the Pub, enjoy my beer and hear the up and coming staffer pitch her little project and ask me for some funding. That, I could have lived with; but looks like she wants to change the world".

Palucci took a long breath and said, "Here is my

suggestion. Pick up a project that is small, doable and can be done in a short timeframe, say within a year. I will help you with that and that will assist with your upward progression within the service".

Palucci was animated and had started gesticulating, "Now, don't get me wrong. All the discussion that we have had this morning is really interesting, academically. I would certainly be interested in looking at your free energy model. We could even get some of our experts take a look at it. But you need to come into the real world. You need to pick a realistic project, not one that is going to change the world".

Meg stayed silent for a moment and gently said, "But Mr. Palucci, isn't that the reason why we all came here in the first place, to change the world and make it a better place?" asked Meg.

Palucci paused mid-air and lowered his hand with a hint of annoyance at having been reminded of a Palucci twenty years earlier.

Meg said, "Okay. I will take up a realistic project for my development programme. But I want to continue exploring the Free Economy Programme. And I want you to be my mentor. I want you to show me how to get this done. You know the people, the processes and how to make this work", said Meg.

"I think you overestimate my capabilities, young lady. But I appreciate where you are coming from. Let

me think about it. By the way thanks for the lunch",
said Palucci as he got up to leave.

CHAPTER 3

The Funeral

Meg woke up to her alarm for a 5:30 start. Today she planned to hit the gym for an hour before going in to work. Flicking through her phone for messages, Meg saw one from Nader. Like any loving brother, Nader would very rarely communicate with her.

Nader's message read, "Morty passed away last night, your time. Sorry".

Meg realized she had been sitting on the rim of the bathtub for a while. She touched her cheeks and realized they were wet and something inside her cracked. Heaving and sobbing into the towel, Meg slowly made way into the bedroom. She certainly did not think she would react so strongly to Morty's demise.

She packed an overnight bag, messaged her team leader and was in the car hitting the Barton Highway in under forty-five minutes. Getting out of Canberra, Meg suddenly realized she did not know Morty's family or even if he had one. It was impulsive. She just had to be there.

Meg wiped her eyes reminding herself to stay alert, for it was a seven-hour drive. Hitting the Hume, Meg went on autopilot, remembering how she had caught up with Morty a couple of times when she had gone back home from the university during semester breaks. Once she had a catch up with Prof. Iyer as well. And she shared some pictures with the rest of the group. Meg wondered if she would see Prof. Iyer this time around.

Entering Gundagai, Meg got off the freeway and pulled into a service station. The rest of the gang had already received the message. Everyone was posting messages of condolences; Meg wasn't sure to whom. Meg texted, "Driving down to farewell Morty".

Getting back on the Hume, Meg wanted to talk, to someone, to everyone. And yes, talking was the better option to texting while driving, Meg reminded herself.

Mindful of the time difference, she called Nader. "Hi dadash", Meg said.

"Hi sis, how's it going", asked Nader.

"I am okay", said Meg.

"Are you driving?" asked Nader.

"Yeah. On the Hume past Gundagai on the way home", said Meg.

"He meant a lot to you, didn't he?" Nader said and continued, "I was a bit shocked myself. Just came out of the blue".

"Yeah, …", Meg trailed.

"Look, watch out and stay safe; it is a long drive. And say hi to everyone over there", Nader signed off.

Meg wondered how Nader had changed from being the atom smash kid he had been.

Nader had moved to the United States following a dream of doing some cutting-edge work in the field of cryptography. For the first few years, things were going well. He was well regarded by his team members and his superiors. He was professionally flying high and seemed excited with his achievements in the work front.

Then the restructures started. Some of the key roles were getting offshored. Nader seemed oblivious to the change. During brief conversations with Meg, he seemed to indicate that the real creative work would stay, and he was right in the thick of it.

Meg did not hear from Nader for a while. When she rang up, he did not seem very talkative. One day he let her know that he had been made redundant and his job had been offshored. He had been looking for work for a few months now. He was struggling to find work that was interesting and in the same pay scale he was in.

Meg realized she had just gone past the Wagga exit. The traffic was slowly building up. Her mind wandered back to Nader. His marriage had broken up and he had moved from New Jersey to New York just across the border. Over the last year, he had taken up what he called a "dead end" job at half the pay. Interestingly, Nader had gotten in touch with Karan who was in New York and apparently it was Karan who had gotten Nader his job.

Since school, Karan had very limited contact with the group. He would respond to Meg's comments in private, rarely. On finishing university, Karan had joined a consultancy firm and had moved to the United States. Nader indicated that Karan was in the energy division of a merchant banking outfit and was doing very well; Karan had been identified as one of the bright minds of the organization and had been placed on an accelerated pathway up the ladder.

Meg was approaching Albury–Wodonga, the state border. As she drove over the Murray river and entered Victoria, she felt a surge of excitement. It was always the same whenever she went back home. It had started drizzling. It was suddenly turning dark with an overcast sky. Meg made sure her headlights were on and raised the heating inside the car. Within half an hour, it was bright and sunny again. Welcome to Victoria, she thought.

The funeral was a solemn affair. Some of Morty's colleagues spoke. Some sadness. Some tears. No one spoke of the Free Ice Cream Project. Meg was surprised to see that Morty had a life outside of the Free Ice Cream Project. Meg noticed Prof. Iyer at the far end of the room. They both nodded at each other.

Later Meg and Prof. Iyer walked across to the café for a coffee. Sitting down, Meg realized that Prof. Iyer seemed to have aged much more in the last few years. She smiled, and he said, "Yes, time seems to have done a number on us older folk. And you have turned out to be a fine young woman".

Meg nodded, smiled and said, "Thanks, how are you?"

"I am going okay", said Prof. Iyer. "I somehow had a feeling that I would see at least one of your group here today. So where is everyone?"

Meg gave him a brief overview of how everyone had dispersed across the globe and what they were doing and where. She then said, "I was surprised that there was no mention of the project today. No one stood up to acknowledge his brainchild".

Prof. Iyer stayed quiet for a while, slowly cleared his throat and said, "Things had not gone well here in the last few years. Since the big presentation, Morty tried to keep the project concept moving. He tried to keep in touch with some of the politicians who seemed to be all for it at the presentation. All of them kept brushing him off. It seems that they were just happy to bask in some limelight but did not really understand the concept. And the few who understood it seemed to think it was farfetched and totally unrealistic".

"Morty tried to keep the concept alive in the local town. People had started to avoid him considering him to be a bore. There was even a rumour floating around that he had lost his marbles.

In the last couple of years, I was probably the only person Morty would talk to. Keep in mind we had been friends for many decades and both of us were well aligned in our thought process in many areas.

Over the last twenty years, both of us had been toying with this idea of making everything free. Over the last few years, Morty and I have been having long dejected conversations on how we have this amazing global solution, and no one is taking it up.

I came to terms with it. Morty struggled. We found the solution for global poverty, but we had a much bigger problem on our hands, understanding people. We had no idea why they did not promote this solution; why they didn't take it up. We were clueless on how to address this.

I repeatedly told Morty that it was not our fight, that it was for the next generation to do it. But Morty did not see it that way. For some reason, he thought we had failed humanity. He continued to hit his head against this community brick wall and that just about killed him".

Driving back to Canberra, the weather was atrocious. It was dark, blowing and hailing. Meg had to pull over, under shelter, to escape the hail damage a few times.

Meg started to talk to herself aloud, "Okay. It is now squarely in our court. No more Morty. Iyer has clearly indicated that it is up to us to make this happen. We will need to decide if we should make this happen or bury this and move on".

She thought for a while and uttered aloud, "Hell, what is this 'we' all about. There is no 'we', it is just me. It is time to stop hiding behind others and looking for excuses. It is time for you to grow up and be an adult. Are you in or out?"

For the next hour, Meg explored her options. She had a plan for her career progression, but she was clear that the free ice cream concept was her passion. She was aware that it was going to be a bumpy ride if she took that path. It was going to be very hard for most part, and there was a high probability of failure. Could she handle a life of failure?

Meg thought for a while and did something brilliant. She decided to restate her goals.

She said to herself, "I will focus my efforts on making the free ice cream concept a reality. That is my goal. I cannot, and I will not fail in this goal. If I can see some success and see some results in my lifetime, that will be great. If not, that is okay too.

However, as part of my effort, I will keep the flame alive. I will engage with the next generation and make sure that this concept is passed on to them. That they will continue the fight after me. I will create a hundred Megs who in turn will create a million Megs, and through sheer numbers, we will make this happen".

As she crossed the Murray, the weather started getting better. Meg's mind also cleared up.

CHAPTER 4

Palucci

Back in Canberra, Meg started going through her files from months and years back. She started pulling all material and analysis that she had done over the years on the Free Ice Cream Economy project. She smiled at the FrICE acronym in her files.

It helped that she was reasonably thorough and disciplined. There was a decent file structure. Most of the extracts had references like details of the websites that she had pulled information from. She started to type.

The goal is to arrive at FrICE. The big steps to get there are to make energy free, metals and plastics free, and then machines free and automated to do all the work. That way there will be no costs and the output can be free.

The first sphere of action was energy. Let us tackle it, she thought and pulled out her old files and notes and references on energy. Meg started listing out the important things that needed to be addressed.

- The project needs to be commercially viable
- The project needs to be commercially attractive for greater public participation
- The project needs to be politically attractive, needs popularity and public support
- The project needs to take care of people impacted by this change, employees in traditional power enterprises

The first item to address was the commercial viability of the project. Meg started going back to her data for information on the indicative cost of building a solar farm. She validated that cost by checking the same with currently available estimates and found the estimates to be reasonably accurate.

She then built up a simplistic business model with some assumptions and ran the numbers. It seemed to stack up. She was aware that this was a rough guestimate; well, this is as "back-of-the-envelope" as you can get, Meg thought, smiling to herself. She then started addressing the other critical requirements for the Free Energy Project by making some notes on additional details.

By the end of the week, Meg decided to make the move. She sent a four-hour meeting request to

Palucci to discuss the Free Energy Project. She also attached a synopsis of the Free Ice Cream Project and the Free Energy business plan she had put together.

As expected, she got a brief and sharp message from Palucci: "Meet me at the café at 3:30", it said. Meg did.

Palucci was getting his coffee. Meg joined him, picked up her coffee and joined Palucci at his table.

"What is going on", asked Palucci.

"It is almost six months since we had a meeting on the Free Ice Cream Project", Meg started.

Palucci let out an exasperated groan and said, "Oh my God, not the Free Ice Cream Project again. Young lady, do you not remember what I told you the last time, to stick to small doable projects that you can actually complete and move ahead?"

Meg nodded in agreement. "Yes, and that was what I have been doing in the last few months. And I will continue to do that. I think I have demonstrated my commitment to that in the last six months".

Palucci waited sensing that Meg was not finished. Meg continued, "I have had a moment of clarity if you may call it that. I accept that the Free Ice Cream Project is huge, that it would take many decades to complete, that we may not see the project to its completion.

However, I have realized that the project is an

integral part of me. I have decided that I am going to progress it as much as I can. If I see results in my lifetime, that would be great. If not, I am okay with that too as long as I have progressed it to a point where others can take it up and run with it. And I need help with this. I am clear that I am way out of my depth here. I need you to guide me, help me, be my mentor for this project".

Palucci was taken aback, not so much by what Meg had said, but what he saw in her eyes. Something had changed. This was not the same young woman who sat before him six months back.

Meg seemed to sense the unasked question and said, "Morty died last week".

"Oh, I am sorry", said Palucci and remained silent.

They both sat in silence and Meg looked up and said, "Yes. That really shook me up. I did not expect it myself", she paused and continued, "All this while, in my mind, it was Morty and Iyer who carried the project and the concept. Now Morty is gone and I suddenly feel the project sitting on my shoulders. It feels like I have inherited it. If I do not do anything, who else will?"

After a longish silence, Palucci said, "Okay. I am with you on this. I will go through the material that you have sent me. But let us be very clear. It does not mean that I am on board. You will have to do a lot of heavy lifting to convince me that we are absolutely not wasting our time. Send me a meeting invite and we will start talking. And by the way, break it up. You are not going to get four-hour chunks".

Meeting with Palucci

They met at the meeting room adjacent to Palucci's office. Meg could look into the garden from where she was sitting.

Meg kicked off the meeting and said, "The goal is to arrive at Free Ice Cream Economy, FrICE for short, where every material thing is free to everyone. The big steps to get there are to", and here Meg started counting with her fingers, "one, to make energy free, and then, to make metals and plastics free, and then, to make machines free and fully automated to do all the work. That way, there will be no costs associated with making anything, and so, the output can be free. Any comments?"

Palucci nodded asking her to go on.

Meg continued, "The first step is to make free energy. I also believe that the energy generated needs to be clean and renewable. We currently have climate change issues due to our emissions. I think we should move away from fossil fuels and transition to clean energy. Further, any energy solution that we propose should be renewable – should have a perennial source that doesn't dry up in the near future".

Palucci nodded in agreement, "Clean renewable energy is preferred, got it. But strictly speaking, your FrICE does not necessarily need clean, renewable energy, but just free energy. Am I correct?"

"Absolutely right", said Meg and continued, "Talking of clean renewable energy, we have a few options. We can explore Solar, Wind, Wave, Geothermal and so on as viable solutions".

"How come you are not considering Nuclear?" asked Palucci.

"Well, I am not eliminating it totally. Nuclear Fusion is not really a proven technology yet. There are a few nuclear fusion initiatives going on around the world. ITER, one of the biggest fusion reactor projects, is planning to be operational in a few years. As they say, fusion will always be a couple of decades away before the technology is proven and available to everyone", Meg smiled using this well-worn cliché on Fusion.

"Nuclear Fission is a different beast; it has a bad rap among people; the Chernobyls and Fukushimas have not helped. But my basic research indicates that the latest Gen-4 reactors are much safer. So, we can add them to the list of potential solutions.

But for the purpose of this model, I explored solar as the potential clean and renewable energy solution. Even in solar, there is solar thermal technology and solar photovoltaic (PV) technology. I have taken up solar PV as the likely solution and have run some numbers on that basis".

"Okay, let us look at this solar model", said Palucci.

"In our scenario, we provide free energy with a solar farm. And we will go into the details of that now", said Meg and continued, "We want this solar farm to be built and operated by Not-for-Profit Organizations, or NFPs. That way once the input costs are eliminated, the organization can provide the generated power for free".

"How come you are going to the private sector. I thought you would want the government to do this", said Palucci.

Meg responded, "Before I jump into the specifics, I would like to table my general approach for FrICE implementation. To successfully implement FrICE, we are going to have many transition projects and initiatives. I think it would be better if they are driven by the market – by the people. It would be better if the transition projects are commercially viable and sustainable and can stand on their own legs. Don't get me wrong. I am not against government intervention or support. I think they are very important to steer the transition initiatives in the right direction. But it would be better if the initiatives ran on their own steam. What do you think?"

Palucci smiled. "You haven't ruled out anything here, have you? You are saying that you would prefer the market to drive the project with government regulation as and where you need it. That is pretty much the current status here and in most of the other countries".

Meg continued, "Okay. We will continue with the market-driven model. The solar farm will be built on borrowed money. We will collect the deposit for the project from the general public. We will offer better than market returns for them on the same. We will borrow the remaining amount from financial institutions as a loan.

The farm will sell the generated electricity. With that revenue, the solar farm will pay off the deposit money to the general public and repay the loans to the financial institutions. Once all the monies have been paid off and the farm is debt free, all electricity produced becomes free".

"That's it?" said Palucci looking puzzled.

"Yes. Here is the draft model with all numbers and projections", Meg referred to a printout on the table.

"Before we jump into the details, let me get this clear", said Palucci. "Your solar farm is going to be built on borrowed money and you are going to pay off the debts with the revenue over a period of time?"

"Yes".

"So, strictly speaking, this is a commercial venture like any other. In which case, your project has to be commercially attractive to investors. Otherwise you will not be able to raise the money".

"Yes", said Meg and continued, "From that perspective, I want these projects to carry lower risk, deliver better than market returns and be commercially attractive for the investors. And I want these projects to have greater public participation as investors".

"I think I agree with you, but I would like to get clarity on your thought process. So, let me ask the question, why?" said Palucci.

"Simple. If any project has a low risk and provides better than market returns, it will be a preferred investment. If the general public get an opportunity to invest in such projects and gain financially, they would love and support those projects. If the public love and support these projects, so will the politicians, and at that point we have the whole nation behind us and supporting FrICE".

"Debatable, but okay. Let me now refine my question. How?" asked Palucci.

Meg said, "Let us consider the issue of business

risk. Let us say a company is interested in building and operating a solar farm. They would put up a business case and go to the market to raise the required capital. What will make the business venture an attractive one?

The first is that the business is a viable one. For this, one of the most important criteria is that the business has a confirmed market to sell their goods, in this case energy. So, if the business has a long-term power purchasing contract with the government, that would be a very good start.

Next, the business will need the know-how and technical expertise to make the product, i.e., operate a solar farm in this case. If the government starts an entity that provides best practice know-how and expertise in building and operating solar farms, to address any knowledge deficit and support the solar farm operators, then that particular risk is also minimized.

The next requirement is for the project to deliver better than market returns and be commercially attractive for the investors. To address this, let us first start looking at my energy proposal", said Meg and started going through the model with Palucci. It was a basic business model and fairly simplistic.

Based on her research, Meg had assessed the capital investment required to build a one-megawatt solar farm. In her model, 30% of the capital investment required was being raised from the general public. The other 70% was being raised as loans from financial institutions. She had indicated that the land could be leased to the NFP for free by the government. That way the land cost would be zero.

Meg had estimated four hours of production per day, allowing for effective daylight times and rainy days. "The projections are in line with my research", Meg said. Based on the same, she had made estimates for power generation per year.

"When we start generating power, we sell it to the market", Meg said. She had applied the estimated feed-in-tariff values and projected revenue accordingly. The revenue was used to repay the Principal and Interest on the loans to the Financial Institutions and the general public. She was offering a higher than market percentage interest for the general public. Running the numbers, her model was able to pay off the loan in less than ten years.

Meg said, "The effective life of a solar farm is around twenty-five years. This debt-repayment model gives us fifteen years of effective life after the farm has been paid off, when we are able to deliver energy for free".

"Are people going to be running the NFPs? Will they be working without any income? Or is that part of the cost of operation?" Palucci peppered her with questions.

"Yes, People will be initially involved in setting up the NFPs. There will be a one-off labour cost associated with this and this can be added to the cost of purchasing the machines and be recovered through the debt-repayment model. Once the NFPs are set up and operational, they should require very few people to run the NFP. By design, it should be fully automated and people free.

The earliest solar farms may not be fully automated. There may still be some labour involved with ongoing operations and maintenance. But that cost would be minimal and the NFP should be able to deliver energy, for almost free, for fifteen years. And as technology improves with enough stimulus, the next gen solar farms will be totally automated and people free and will deliver energy for free, post pay off".

Palucci said, "Okay. Another issue. You want to offer a higher than market percentage interest for the general public. If this project is going to deliver everything for free, what is the point of offering money to people? How will that entice people?"

"FrICE transition will take some time. We are not going to get everything for free tomorrow. My analysis indicates it would take a few decades to get there. During that time, money will still play a part in society. On day one of the project kicking off, nothing will be different. We will all still pay for what we need as we had been doing yesterday. Gradually, as the project progresses, we will see things getting cheaper and eventually becoming free.

So, to answer your question, yes, money will matter to people during the transition, which may take between thirty to fifty years to be completed", said Meg.

"So, are we going to use this debt-repayment model forever?" asked Palucci.

"Only till our solar panels become free", said Meg. Seeing Palucci's confused look Meg said, "To manufacture any item we need energy, machines, labour and raw materials. Correct?" Palucci nodded.

"In the case of the solar farm, we do not need energy to run; we actually generate energy. We do not pay for the input raw material which is the sun light; it is for free. Our only cost is to buy the solar panels. When the panels become free, there will be no cost and the solar farm will be free".

"And how do the panels become free?" asked Palucci.

"The panels will become free when the raw materials for the panels, the metals, synthetics and glass become free; when the factory, with all required machines, that make these panels, becomes free; and when the energy required to run the factory becomes free.

The whole FrICE transition is about how to make the machines free. We need machines to make machines. We identified this as the main paradox when we did this project in school. Throughout this FrICE transition, we will kick off with commercial models and gradually get to the point where machines become free.

As the energy machines become free, energy becomes totally free. We need money only to buy the machines and with free solar panels, we will not need the money; we will not need the ten–fifteen debt-repayment model anymore.

Similarly, as mining machines become free, all metal ore becomes totally free. We needed money only to buy the mining machines and we will not need the commercial debt-repayment model anymore.

When all machines are free, the FrICE transition is complete and everything will be free for everyone from then onwards", Meg concluded.

Palucci let out a long sigh and said, "Sounds good. Maybe too good to be true. I need to sleep over this to get some clarity. Let us continue this another day".

***

Back at his desk, Palucci realized that Meg had organized for short sessions over the next few weeks to continue discussing FrICE. Palucci accepted the meeting invites.

Over the next few weeks, Palucci and Meg discussed a range of issues related to FrICE. They went through the process of FrICE for energy, mining, metal and other manufacturing industries and agriculture, in detail.

There was discussion on how to get a commercial company to transition to FrICE. "A commercial company's primary goal is to make a profit for its shareholders. How do we get them to move away from that and become a not-for-profit?" was the key question. They tried exploring various tacks and did not come up with a good solution on the same. The easiest seemed to be through use of force – manipulation of mining codes or using government directives. Both Meg and Palucci were not happy with that option and agreed that it was an open end to be resolved.

The issue of job losses and transitioning people through this change took a couple of sessions. Palucci had a few questions and Meg painted a picture of the possible solutions. They had detailed discussions on how a FrICE transaction would work. They also discussed peripheral and related issues such as the impact of FrICE on the use of money, taxation, economic valuation and metrics.

At the end of these sessions, Palucci said, "We are certain on some aspects and reasonably comfortable with some solutions. And we do not know the answer for a few. That is our current status. Correct?"

Meg nodded in agreement.

"I think we have enough to take it forward. I want you to put together a presentation that paints the big picture; what is FrICE, why we need to do it and how we should do it. I will corral representatives from the secretariat, from the relevant ministries, and we will start the conversation. These are smart people who also have the expertise in their particular areas. And we have enough to put on the table for this group to consider.

We will present this to them as is, be upfront that we don't have all the answers and we want them to contribute and to join us in unravelling this complex problem. I am sure they will come up with some solutions", said Palucci.

Meg became mindful of the shift from you to we; Palucci had come around.

CHAPTER 6

FrICE – The Slingshot

The board room was slowly filling up. Secretaries, Under-Secretaries and Additional-Secretaries from various departments and ministries had gathered and were taking their seats. Palucci was shaking hands and making small talk with them. Meg was standing next to the screen fidgeting with the PowerPoint clicker. She had dressed up for the occasion.

Palucci started addressing the attendees. "Thanks for coming", he started. "Almost a decade back, a bunch of school kids were in the news. They had found a way to make everything free for everyone. I am sure most of you remember that". Heads nodded. "Some of us gave it a look. True, the concept was big; it involved complete transformation of the global economy. But, to be fair, none of us could find fault with the logic. Interestingly, almost all economists decided to stay quiet on this theory that was put forward by these kids". Palucci paused and with a flourish said,

"Here we have one of those school kids", pointing to Meg.

There was palpable silence with a few raised eyebrows indicating mild astonishment. Palucci registered it and said with a smile, "I know. For most of us it feels like it was yesterday". Palucci paused and continued, "Meg has joined our team and is one of our junior staffers. Sometime back, during one of our discussions, Meg brought up this topic of free everything; how all material things can be made for free. As a diligent mentor worth his salt, I duly advised her to drop it and focus on something that is doable. But she was persistent and over a few sessions has drawn me into it.

Let me be clear. We do not have all the answers. We are going to table this idea and will want your expertise to unravel some of the complex issues.

I have asked Meg to kick off the presentation with an overview of the process – how to make everything free for everyone. I concede that you are one of the smartest bunch of people I know. However, the idea is fairly radical. It questions most of our ingrained, deeply held, beliefs and opinions. My first reaction when I heard it was to shoot it down and many of you might feel that way.

We will go through this presentation today. I want you all to go away and think about it for a couple of weeks. I want you to consider the issue and form a position on the same; is it critical? Should we act on it now? Or can we take it easy and defer any action to later?

I also want you to explore the process and identify key challenges in your area and how to address the same. What would you need from other portfolios to make it happen?

Once we have done that, I will organize individual sessions with each and every one of you to discuss these in detail. We can all convene once we have gone through these steps. How does that sound?"

"Sounds okay to me. However, let us not make too many assumptions. Let's hear what we came in for today and we can then see if we need to go through all of these steps", responded Ivan the additional energy secretary.

Palucci nodded in agreement, turned to Meg and said, "All yours".

"Thank you", Meg said to Palucci and turned to the room. "Thanks for coming this afternoon. As Mr. Palucci suggested, I would like to take you through the Free Ice Cream Economy concept very briefly. We refer to it as FrICE in short.

Most manufactured goods are made in factories. In these factories, machines work on raw materials to make these things, be it a fridge, a TV, an umbrella, a cup of ice cream or a pair of shoes, right?"

Heads nodded.

"Businesses make these things and sell it to us for a price and that becomes their revenue. However, the businesses also incur costs to make these things. Costs like labour cost, raw material cost, energy cost and the cost to build the factory in the first place. It is the same in agriculture as well. There are costs involved in raising a crop of rice, wheat or apples. The revenue less cost is the profit that the business makes.

Now if we were to eliminate all of those costs, the business can sell the TV or the umbrella or the can of milk for one cent and still make a profit. Further, if the business were to be a not-for-profit organization, it can give all of these farmed or manufactured items for free and still be sustainable; no revenue, but no cost as well and hence the organization can continue its farming or manufacturing activity forever. The trick is, how do we eliminate all those costs? We will go through that process in some detail later in the presentation.

Before I get to that, I would like to highlight two reasons on why we need to take this concept seriously and act on this today.

The first is the issue of massive job losses at the global level and the associated disruption it is going to cause if we don't do anything about it. FrICE addresses this issue and proposes a viable solution.

One of the major issues that people face is the issue of job loss. What was once considered as a stable industry is suddenly impacted and goes through a major disruption. It could be because of new disruptive technology or migration of jobs from developed to developing nations, following lower cost of labour.

This has caused unrest among the impacted population in the developed countries. The concept of a skill for life or a job in a company for life is gone. People are forced to constantly adapt, learn new skills and enter a new job market or perish. Not everyone has been able to make the transition effectively. Many struggle to adapt. Some perish.

The political leadership has not been very effective on this transition, telling people that jobs go where labour is cheap, but not really providing the impacted masses with any reasonable transition plan or support. Some unscrupulous political opportunists even claim to bring the jobs back, building walls and closing borders. It has been a nightmare of a transition that has facilitated a Trump and a Brexit.

Under this scenario creeps along the silent killer juggernaut – Automation and Artificial Intelligence (AI). While this is being talked about, no one seems to have a viable solution with respect to the associated job loss. Conservative estimates peg it at 20 to 30 million jobs lost by 2030. Unfortunately, this may even become a catchy slogan. And this time around, it would not just be the developed countries who would be impacted, the developing countries will feel the pain as well.

With the advent of automation and AI in almost all facets of life, in the foreseeable future, we will be in a position where the majority of the population will be jobless. Many of them will be unemployable and can be classed as 'useless' from an economic perspective. And the best solution being proposed to counter this is the wishful thinking that something else will come along".

Palucci stepped in and said, "Let me use an analogy to get the story across. As a society, we are bobbing along in a canoe, in this dangerous river of progress. Over the last few decades, we have gone over some rapids and that was not pretty. Offshoring manufacturing to countries with cheap labour and associated loss of manufacturing jobs in developed nations were painful, but it is just a taste of things to come. We can hear impending automation as the roaring sound of the waterfall downstream. We know that the particular waterfall is a potential killer. Some in the canoe are furiously trying to paddle back, trying to stop progress, close doors, stop trade, stop offshoring, go back to the pre-automation days. Others in the canoe are transfixed, like rabbits caught in the headlights, waiting for the fall, hoping that something will come along and save them.

FrICE addresses this issue head on. It shows how to effectively navigate this issue and take care of the impacted people during this transition.

Instead of trying to slow down this impending change, FrICE proposes that we accelerate automation, use that change to slingshot ourselves over this killer waterfall and safely land in the calm waters further downstream.

FrICE shows how the post-transition world can be glorious; a world where machines serve and take care of human material needs; a world where humans are relieved of mundane repetitive tasks; a world where we are able to utilize the collective brain power of over 7 billion heads, relieved from mundane tasks, to discover and create new and amazing things".

CHAPTER 7

Atlantis

Meg started, "The second reason why it is critical for us to implement FrICE at the earliest is the issue of economic slavery. Countries that implement FrICE become dominant and powerful while the laggards end up being subservient. Let us take a look.

Let us say, Atlantis, our mythical country, has managed to successfully implement FrICE. Atlantis is now able to farm or manufacture all items cost free. Atlantis gives all items for free to all of its citizens and exports the surplus.

Let us say our country manufactures umbrellas at a dollar each. The best we can do is to sell it at a dollar each and make no profit. However, we can buy it from Atlantis at eighty cents an umbrella, because Atlantis can sell it at any cost and still make money; their cost is zero.

The same applies to all things we consume, be it medicines, military ware, cosmetics, food, machines, appliances and so on. We cannot commercially compete with Atlantis and we will buy everything off them as it makes better financial sense. What also happens is that our farming and manufacturing capabilities die a natural death through this process.

Over a period of time, our infrastructure required for these farming or manufacturing activities will vanish as they are not being used; the competencies and skillsets required for these activities will be lost as well; people move on to other things or other places. With infrastructure dying out and losing relevant skills and competencies, it becomes all the more difficult to restart any of these activities, that have shutdown, if we wish to do so at a later date.

Atlantis now has a significant competitive advantage over us in the global market place. We have lost our capacity to grow our food or manufacture things that we need. At this point, Atlantis can dictate terms and gain a position of economic dominance. They can increase the price of goods and produce. When we, the recipient country, get frustrated and decide to restart our manufacturing base, we will struggle. It might take decades and significant political capital to do the same.

What is interesting is that half way through our initiative to restart our manufacturing, Atlantis can effectively drop the price at any point and kill our initiative to rebuild our industry. Atlantis can keep playing this game for a long time, ensuring we will be dependent on them for all farmed and manufactured goods, maintaining their economic dominance over us".

Palucci stepped in and said, "We are all aware of the fact that economic dominance facilitates and leads to political and militaristic dominance. It is interesting to note that it is not just the number of nuclear warheads that determines a super power. It is the economic dominance that leads to dominance in other spheres. A military super power may have the capacity to destroy but FrICE super power has the ability to create and that will always win.

However, it will be a sad fact that with a depleted manufacturing capability, we will be no match for Atlantis, in terms of military power and strength. We will not have the capacity to make any military hardware while they will have more than sufficient capacity to do so.

Further, if you are thinking that we will be dominant in the creative domain while Atlantis is focused on making material things, think again. Through FrICE, Atlantis has gained economic dominance. They are in a good financial position taking money from us for things that cost them nothing. And their people are not slaving in factories producing things; all production facilities have been automated as part of the FrICE solution. Unlike our citizens, they have a citizenry with money in their pockets and time in their hands to focus on education, enhancing their knowledge base and delivering creative solutions".

Meg concluded, "So, it is evident that adopting FrICE early makes a country a dominant global force – economically, politically and militaristically. If we are not one of the early adopters, we risk global subservience".

Palucci proposed a break. In the restroom, one was heard commenting, "Sounds logical and scary". Another responded, "It felt more like a script for a scary movie".

Yet another commented, "We need to go through this scenario in some more detail. We wouldn't shutdown or offshore all activities, would we? We will retain what is deemed critical".

"In this scenario, even if we decide to retain the critical stuff, say we decide to make our own arms, the nuts and bolts and components will come from Atlantis and we will still be dependent on them; they can have us by our proverbial if they decide to do so", replied another voice.

"The only reason we are losing manufacturing currently is because of the labour cost. If we eliminate the labour cost, then we are on equal footing with any other country", said one.

"And if we eliminate the labour, then what are our people going to do? Where are the jobs? And why will the politicians be interested, if there are no votes behind this?" responded another.

"Guys, I think Palucci was right in asking us to let it sink in. Let us get back. I want to see how this FrICE thing is going to unfold".

And they did.

CHAPTER 8

FrICE — The Paradox

"We will kick off from the basic premise", Meg said once all the attendees had settled down post break. "The key costs for a manufacturing or agricultural business are the cost of raw material, labour, energy and capital cost of the factory or machines. We will look at the cost of raw material first.

Typically, raw material for one business is the output or finished product of another business. Wheat is the farm output and is the raw material for a flour mill. The flour is the output of the mill which in turn is the input for a bakery that makes bread and so on.

Similarly, ore, the output of a mine, is the input raw material for a metal factory. The metal from the metal factory is the input raw material for a factory making metal components. The metal components are in turn the input raw materials for a factory making machines and so on.

So, when we make a business cost free, the

output of that business has zero cost and becomes free raw material for the business downstream. Thus, we can eliminate the raw material input cost for all manufacturing and agricultural business.

Next, let us consider the cost of labour. With the development of automation and AI in the industry, it is inevitable that all manufacturing and agricultural processes will become fully automated and labour free in the foreseeable future. All businesses are focused on reducing cost and the global industry is going this way. This accelerated change is already getting people worried on the future of the jobs market. As part of FrICE, we will propose initiatives to further accelerate complete automation of all manufacturing and agricultural processes and make them labour free, thus eliminating labour cost. For those wondering what will happen to people and jobs, we will address it later.

Next item to address is energy. We are at a point that any discussion on energy must recognize the impact of fossil fuel on climate change. Hence, for any further discussion, let us exclude fossil fuels as a source of energy; let us only consider clean, renewable energy sources.

As a business, energy generation has cost impacts. Cost of raw material is not an issue for solar or wind-based power generators; it is the sunlight or wind and they are for free. Further, all power generation facilities can be fully automated, thus removing the cost of labour. Energy as an input will not be a cost issue as these facilities generate energy. The only remaining cost issue is the cost of the facility, the cost of the power-generating machines. As such, if the power-generating machines are made free, the generated power will be free.

So, let us follow this thread and figure out the costs involved with machines. Machines are predominantly made of metal; some synthetic materials like plastics are also used. They are made in factories. Like other businesses, the factories have energy cost, cost of raw materials, cost of labour and capital cost of the factory or machines.

Considering the energy cost, we have a circular relationship. We need free energy machines to make energy free of cost and we need free energy to make machines free of cost.

Considering the cost of the factory, we have another circular relationship. We need free machines to make machines free. Before we consider the other cost impacts, the logical aberration becomes apparent; we enter this circular logical chicken and egg paradox".

Meg paused, looked around and said, "The reason I have been giving this preview is because of this paradox. There is a way out of this. But when I take you through the two-step process, it is important for you to have an awareness of this paradox and that we are taking the two-step process to overcome the same".

"Once again, I am not sure where we are going or why, but let us keep going and we will respond at the end", said Ivan. Others nodded in agreement. Palucci nodded to Meg asking her to go on.

CHAPTER 9

FrICE – Energy

Meg started diving into her explanation of the FrICE solution.

"Let us start our FrICE solution. We are focused on delivering free energy to the economy. While it is not essential to the FrICE solution, with the advent of climate change, and fossil fuel's contribution to the same, we take this opportunity to design our FrICE solution based on clean renewable energy. I have selected solar as the energy solution for the FrICE business case".

Meg flicked on to the next slide and continued, "We invite NFPs [Not-for-Profit Organizations] to establish solar farms. We offer them suitable crown land on free lease, thus reducing their capital investment.

We contract power purchase agreements with the NFPs at the outset, thus providing stability and making it a minimal risk venture. We will also set up a centre of excellence that is able to support, guide and mentor the NFPs on establishing and operating solar farms. This will address any technical deficit at the NFP and further reduce the risk profile of the new venture, helping the NFP to successfully raise capital.

We set up the programme such that public participation drives this infrastructure development. The NFPs can raise the deposit, say 30% of the project value, from the general public. The NFPs raise the remaining funds as commercial loans from financial institutions.

We design the programme such that the NFPs will pay a better than market rate as interest to the public investors. This will make sure that these projects are well received and are viewed favourably by the general public. This public support will be crucial in making this project a political positive. It is only when people are behind these initiatives that we have a decent chance of success", Meg nodded her head towards Palucci acknowledging his contribution.

Palucci turned to others and said, "Yes, I insisted that she put it in there. If we are going to look at something this big, we better have people loving it and supporting us; else we don't stand a chance".

Heads nodded in agreement.

Meg continued, "We also make sure that the NFP business model puts aside some money towards a fund to support the impacted people. People who work in traditional energy industries are the ones who will be predominantly impacted by this shift to renewables. They need to be supported through this transition and this fund will assist with the same".

Meg could see a few attendees rapidly taking notes.

"Based on these factors, I have run some basic numbers and they seem to stack up. We are looking at a solar farm generating power for four hours a day, on an average. We assume no cost associated with use of Land. We assume that the Plant will be predominantly automated and people free. For the revenue estimates, we have used a feedback tariff value close to the current market value. The revenue is used to repay the debt, principal and interest, as well as top up the industry transition fund.

Under such a model and with these assumptions and numbers, the NFP is able to repay the debt in under ten years. Typically, these Plants have an effective life of around twenty-five years. Once the debt has been repaid, all power generated by this solar farm is available for free for the next fifteen years.

And we have free energy", Meg concluded.

Meg continued, "As Mr. Palucci mentioned, we have limited ourselves to painting the big picture, for this session. A lot more detail needs to go into this to make it a solid proposal".

"And that was what we wanted to do", stepped in Palucci. "I did not want Meg to go much deeper into this proposal by herself. She could effectively spend her whole life trying to collect supporting data and possibly be barking up the wrong tree. I think there is enough here as a concept. I think it is time for us to put our collective heads and make an assessment if this stacks up as a viable concept".

CHAPTER 10

FrICE – Mining

Meg flicked across to the next slide that said mining. "Before we jump into the mining solution, let us look back at why we are going down this way – why energy first and then mining. For our energy solution, the only cost was the cost of the machines. If the solar panels would have been at zero cost, then the solar farm would have been at zero cost and the power generated would have been free for all from day one".

"Aren't you forgetting the cost of installing and commissioning the solar farm?" asked a voice from the audience.

"Well, not really. The expectation of FrICE is that AI-enabled robots will take care of that. When we put out a tender, this requirement will be clearly spelled out. Installation of the solar panels and commissioning the solar farm will need to be automated, done by robots with free energy input. The successful NFP will have the most automation and least cost in this area. Of course, we do not expect the first solar farm installation to be completely automated, but it will happen subsequently", said Meg.

Meg continued, "Cost of machines is the only thing keeping us from making energy free from day one. So, our priority now is to make the machines free. We know that machines are made of metals and some synthetic material like plastics. The metals and plastics are used as raw materials in factories to make these machines. So, we are going to target metals first.

Metals are predominantly dug up and processed by the mine to deliver metal ore. The metal ore is further processed in metal factories to extract the metal. The extracted metal is used as raw material in factories to make the machines that we need.

So, in order to get machines free, one of the things we will need to do is to make the metal free and in turn the metal ore free. Hence, mining follows energy. Once we address mining, we will address metal manufacturing. Does the sequence logic make sense?"

It did.

"Mining throws up a few complications", said Palucci. "When we considered putting up new solar farms, it was reasonably easy; we could put up a solar farm in a place that was sunny and where we had free land available. But mining poses a complexity. We cannot go and mine for, say iron ore or copper, anywhere. We have to mine where the ore deposits are present. And many of these deposits have been identified by commercial mining companies. In many cases, they have existing mining operations going on or they have staked a claim in an identified ore deposit.

We explored various options to get the commercial mining industry into FrICE. We looked at giving free energy to the mines and taking a proportional percentage of production output, a la barter system of sorts. We then explored the option of selling the energy generated to other industries and buying ore from the mining company with that money, a la commercial transaction.

We also considered the option of using the money from energy sales to buy mining machines from the market. But eventually, we came to the issue; if we were to present free equipment and free energy to existing mining companies, there was no guarantee that they would, in turn, deliver the ore for free. Their core interest would be to maximize the profits to their shareholders.

We considered buying controlling interest in a mining company and that was fraught with issues as well. With controlling interest, we could have forced the company to go the FrICE way. However, the value of the shares would have dropped in the market and the minority shareholders would have been justified in taking legal action, asking us for compensation. That, in turn, would have had the same impact as buying the whole company – all the shares, not just a controlling interest.

That led us to the next option of buying a mining company. For this exercise, we have taken the same approach that we took to starting a solar farm. We will invite NFPs to express interest in building and operating a fully automated mine, through a tender process. The NFP will raise 30% of the required capital, for buying a mine and fully automated machines to run it, from the general public and the remaining from commercial lenders.

The mining NFPs will be provided with free energy from our FrICE solar farms. The NFPs will not be charged any royalty for the ore. They will not incur any import duties for fully automated mining machinery. Being a not-for-profit organization, taxes will not apply to them. The operation will be people free as the plant is fully automated. With no input raw material cost, i.e., no royalty, no labour cost due to fully automated machinery and no energy cost as energy is provided for free by the FrICE solar farm, the NFPs will have no operational cost.

The NFPs will sell the ore, and the revenue will be used to repay the loans, principal and interest. We estimate the mine to fully retire their debts in less than ten years. Once the loans are repaid, the mine becomes totally cost free and all ore mined is provided to downstream FrICE metal manufacturers as free raw material".

The question came from the floor. "How are you making the assumption that you will be able to retire all debts in ten years? You may look at mining as just digging and shovelling but mining is such a varied activity. The mining process, operating costs and capital investment required for an iron ore mine is likely to be different to a coal mine and so will the revenues", said the Under-Secretary from ministry of resources.

George from Treasury stepped in and said, "What we are talking about is the value of a company and how fast we can pay off the debt. Currently, we have varied methods and metrics for valuation: discounted cash flow analysis, earnings multipliers and so on. But these companies that you guys are talking of have no costs. As such, earnings multipliers do not make sense. With no costs, all revenue can be used to pay off the debt plus interest.

Now, let us use a simple revenue multiplier as the company valuation metric. Typically, valuations are between one to three times the actual revenue across industries. It could go as low as half times revenue for slow-growing low potential businesses and up to five times revenue for high growth potential businesses.

Even at the valuation of five times revenue, the operator can repay the debt, with interest, over seven years. So, the debt-repayment model over ten years is a very reasonable assumption for any industry".

"Are we saying that with this debt-repayment model, any manufacturing business can transition from selling the output to providing it for free in ten years' time?" asked Ivan.

"That is correct", said George.

CHAPTER 11

FrICE – Bootstrap

Meg continued, "The next industry to address after mining is metal manufacturing. We adopt a similar approach for the downstream metal manufacturers. They will be operated by NFPs and be funded by the people and commercial lenders. There will be no tax burden as they are an NFP. They will be provided free land for the factory and will be exempt from import duties for fully automated machinery like blast furnaces, crucibles and so on. They will receive free energy from the FrICE power plant and free ore from the FrICE mine".

With no input raw material cost due to free ore, no labour cost due to fully automated machinery and no energy cost due to free energy provided by the FrICE solar farm, the metal manufacturing NFPs will have no operational cost.

The metal manufacturing NFPs will sell the metal and the revenue will be used to repay the loans, principal and interest. As George confirmed, the debt will be fully retired in less than ten years. Once the loans are repaid, the operation becomes totally cost free and all of the manufactured metal is provided downstream to the Shuru factories as free raw material to make machines.

Palucci must have sensed something. He stepped in and commented, "Shuru factories are the primary factories that make machines to build all the other factories. Let us take sugar as an example. Sugar is made in a factory, typically called a Sugar Mill. For us to build this Sugar Mill, we need all the machines that make up the Sugar Mill. The Shuru factory is the primary factory, or factories, that manufacture these machines that make up a Sugar Mill".

Meg clarified what Shuru meant by adding, "Many years ago, in school, we drew lots to have a name for these primary factories. This was the name that got selected and it has stuck. By the way, Shuru means origin or start in some of the languages in the Indian subcontinent".

Meg carried on, "Now, plastic is the other raw material required to make machines. Plastic manufacturing is a four-step process. You drill and extract crude oil using oil rigs or offshore platforms. You then heat it up and cool it, in oil refineries, to extract whatever hydrocarbon you want. You then heat up different hydrocarbons in the presence of a catalyst and cool them to make plastic in petrochemical factories. And then you heat up the plastic beads, pour in moulds and cool it to make the plastic component you want in plastic-moulding factories.

We take a similar approach of ore and metal manufacturing to manufacture plastics. NFPs will operate cost-free oil rigs, oil refineries and petrochemical factories to produce free outputs; crude oil will become the free input raw material to the oil refinery; the hydrocarbons produced will become the free input raw material to the petrochemical factory; and the plastic produced will become the free input raw material to the Shuru factories to make machines.

These fully automated, labour-free, Shuru factories use the free energy, free metal and plastics to make all the machines that we need to kick start FrICE.

Now that our Shuru factories are up and running and are able to make cost-free machines, the primary focus is to build factories to make industry-specific machines. Let us call these the Gen-2 factories.

We start off by building Gen-2 factories that make electricity-generating equipment – solar panels, wind Turbines, Gas Turbines, fuel cells, etc. NFPs that start new electricity-generating facilities will receive free machines from these factories and will not need any funding for capital. There will be no debt to be repaid. They can generate electricity and deliver it for free, from day one.

Our Shuru factories will then make Gen-2 factories that make mining equipment – shovels, winders, haul trucks, crushers, mills and so on. NFPs and other mining companies that become a part of the FrICE fraternity will receive fully automated, people-free mining equipment, from Shuru, for free. They will not need any funding for capital. There will be no debt to be repaid. They can dig and deliver ore for free from day one.

Our Shuru factories will then make Gen-2 factories that make metal manufacturing equipment like blast furnaces, ovens, crucibles and so on. NFPs will receive fully automated, people-free, metal manufacturing factories from Shuru, for free. They will get free raw material, the ore, from the FrICE mine and free energy from the FrICE power plant. With all inputs for free, these factories will deliver free metal from day one to all the Shuru factories.

It will be the same story with plastics.

And with that we have effectively closed the loop and bootstrapped the free economy. Our fully automated Shuru factories will now get truly free raw materials like metal and plastic and free energy to make all the machines that we need", Meg paused looking around.

Some of the audience had a distant look in their faces – some puzzled, some furiously scribbling notes while one was absently chewing her pencil. Palucci called for a break.

In the break room over sandwiches and coffee, comments wafted around. "What about the people?" was one, when another responded, "Well, what about the jobs?"

"It is a very broad scaffold that needs to be covered", said one. "A lot of holes to fill", another agreed as they slowly made their way back to the presentation.

CHAPTER 12

FrICE, Close the Loop

Meg kicked off the session saying, "Now that the machines are free, we are in the FrICE loop where we can make any material thing for free. While there are many avenues from here, let us just take one as an example and see how it will pan out.

Let us take the example of ice cream. Working backwards, to make ice cream, we will need milk, cream and sugar as raw materials. We will need a factory to process the raw materials and make it, and we will need energy to run the factory.

From now on, all factories being built will be fully automated and will not need people. Automation, AI and machine learning are already well developed. Going forward, in this free economy, the need for fully automated factories will be a requirement and will need to be incentivized. Once full automation is promoted and kicks off, it will become the new industrial norm; all new machines and factories will be designed and made to be fully automated and will have the ability to mesh with and participate in the wider automation network, be it factory-wide, city-wide or global.

Getting back to our ice cream, we only need the raw materials, the factory and energy to run the fully automated factory – no people required.

In this case, our Shuru factories will make the equipment required for an ice cream factory – silos, tanks, pumps, motors, gearboxes, churns, chillers, compressors, homogenizers, pasteurizers and so on. Generic standard configuration design templates will be used to build modular assemblies that can readily interface with other modules. The factories will be assembled by robots. And we have our free factory ready.

We have already seen our Shuru factories making electricity-generating equipment – solar panels, wind turbines, gas turbines, fuel cells, etc. So, the power sector has the free generation capacity and is able to supply free energy to our ice cream factory.

Taking a look at the raw materials required, cane sugar is a manufactured commodity. Sugar cane is raised as an agricultural crop and harvested at the sugarcane plantation. The juice is extracted from the cane in the Sugar Mill which is a factory that makes sugar. The extracted juice is then heated up to crystallize the sugar.

Following the thread, we next look at the requirements of the sugarcane plantation. The primary needs are fully automated machines for farm activities such as sowing and harvesting. The farm also requires fertilizer and water to grow the crop.

Our Shuru factories will make free automated machines for all agricultural needs like tractors and combine harvesters.

Our Shuru factories will make automated desalination plants for deficit water when rains fail, or water is insufficient.

Our Shuru factories will make fully automated fertilizer factories which in turn will make the required fertilizer and feed the sugarcane plantation".

Meg paused for a moment and said, "You may note that we have made the sugarcane plantation cost free. However, we have also made all agricultural activity cost free. On day one, we can only support a few farms providing them with free farm machines, free energy, supplemental water and fertilizer. But over a period of time, FrICE will make all farm activity cost free. Wheat, rice, corn, millet, apples, oranges, all agricultural crops are free.

Coming back to sugar, the Shuru factories will make equipment required for the Sugar Mill – rollers, pumps, motors, gearboxes, evaporators, fugals and so on. As with other factories, generic standard configuration design templates will be used to build modular assemblies that can readily interface with other modules. The factories will be assembled by robots, and we have our free Sugar Mill ready. With free energy, no labour and free sugarcane from the plantation, the Sugar Mill is able to manufacture and deliver sugar, for free, to our ice cream factory.

The next raw material ingredient required for our ice cream is milk and cream. Milk is sourced from a dairy farm. The dairy farm needs water to raise its own cattle feed, a milk shed and related equipment to milk, cool and transport the milk to consumers and energy to run the dairy farm.

We have already seen our Shuru factories making electricity-generating equipment to supply free energy. Our Shuru factories have also made fully automated farm machines and fully automated desalination plants. That will take care of the farm equipment and water needs for our cattle feed. The Shuru factories will make equipment required for a fully automated dairy farm.

Our Shuru factories will also make automated health care systems, including drones, that conduct inspections on cattle, administer medication, and expedite quarantine or hospitalization of the animal, as required. Thus, the dairy operation is people free and the milk is produced for free.

You may also note that we have made animal husbandry a cost-free activity. We have a cost-free dairy farm. We can also create cost-free cattle, sheep and poultry farms to produce meat. Earlier we saw that FrICE has made all grain and agricultural produce grown cost free. Now we see that animal husbandry is cost free as well. We can apply the same to even fruits and vegetables. As one of my classmates used to say, 'If you have software to recognize faces why can't we have drones picking the fruit or vegetable at the right condition?'" Meg smiled.

Palucci stepped in and said, "At this point, FrICE has made all food absolutely free. We are able to produce as much food as we need and eliminate global hunger, for sure".

Meg continued, "The remaining raw material is cream which is made in a milk processing factory. With free energy and free milk, the Shuru factory needs to build a fully automated milk processing factory that can make milk powder, butter cheese and cream among other milk-based products.

Thus, our fully automated ice cream factory, that was built by the Shuru factories and is run by the free energy provided, gets cream, milk and sugar as free raw materials to produce free ice cream that everyone gets for free".

Meg finished with a flourish.

Palucci asked the floor for comments.

"There are a few things that need to be resolved. We need clarity on some aspects", said Ivan.

"I agree", said Palucci, "When we discussed this, I was clear. I told Meg that she had something here, a potentially viable concept. I also told her that there is no way one person can run with this on their own. They will spend the rest of their lives trying to gather and analyse the data and generate a reasonable case for the concept. And the more important point is that they will not have the expertise or experience in all of these areas. It was certainly time to go to the experts.

And you guys are the experts. I think we have sufficient information here to trigger a discussion. However, we want you to take a look and decide if there is something in this concept, pick holes in the theory, fill the gaps and provide answers to some of the complex issues.

We have gone as far as we can, and should, on our own. It is time to stop flying solo. This will become a massive initiative, if found viable. We have to pull this together as a team. That is the only way forward", said Palucci.

Everyone agreed.

Palucci continued, "Just a comment, by the way, I have already received three messages from the cabinet wanting to know what the hell is going on in here? One has even made a mention of our first session on the risk of not doing FrICE. As we all know, this is the country's capital; there are no secrets here. I expect a few of you to be getting similar messages. We should expect further interest in this space from our political masters very soon.

So, here is my suggestion. I request you all to have a think about the discussion today. Meg will send you all the presentation material and notes. Please collect your thoughts, specifically on aspects relevant to your ministry. I will ask Meg to book some time with each and every one of you over the next two weeks. Let us take it to the next level of detail and then get together again in two weeks' time. We should be able to make a call on whether we go ahead with this project at that meeting. Any comments?"

There was none. All seemed in agreement.

CHAPTER 13

Energy Issues

Meg entered Ivan's office and met with Ivan's secretary who took her to the meeting room. Presently Ivan entered the room and said, "Right, let us kick off. Why solar?"

"Well, when I started this discussion with Mr. Palucci, I had started looking at available clean energy options listing out solar, wind, wave, geothermal and a range of other power generation options including nuclear fission and fusion as possible options.

I then took up solar PV as the likely solution because it is clean and renewable. It is certainly scalable; you can install a small solar unit at your house, or you could go big and install a huge solar farm, supplying power to a whole city, in what we call the utility scale. It also has one of the lowest capital costs. And the cost per unit of power it generates is also low.

So, I ran some numbers on solar and it seemed to stack up. And to be fair, it was a lot of effort getting the data and analysing on my own in my spare time. Even after all that effort, I had this lingering doubt whether the data I was using was current or even correct and if the methodology I was using for the analysis was the right one".

Ivan said, "Looks like we are not limiting ourselves to solar, then".

"No, we aren't. That was the one I took as a case study to validate this hypothesis and it sort of stacks up, reasonably", Meg finished lamely.

"I agree, the devil is always in the detail and that will bring us to the assumptions you have made", said Ivan. "Have you looked at the limitations of solar, the fact that it is intermittent? We know the sun doesn't shine all the time. And then there are rainy days and cloud cover".

"I sure did. One option is to go for a combination of solar and wind. Looks like wind power is more dominant in night times and will address some of this intermittency", said Meg.

"Yes and no", said Ivan. "It will offset some of the impact, but the issue of intermittency does not go away. Before we look at energy storage options, let us consider the average time that a solar unit will generate power. For our calculation purpose, we can take it as around four hours per day?" Meg nodded.

"Let us say we are replacing a coal-fired power station of one megawatt capacity, with solar. The coal-fired power station will generate power for twenty-four hours generating twenty-four megawatts of power per day. Correct?" Ivan continued. Meg agreed once again.

"A solar farm of one megawatt capacity, generating for four hours a day will only generate four megawatts of power per day. In effect, we may need six times the generating capacity and install facilities that generate six megawatts of solar power to replace one megawatt of coal power.

Now let us look at the storage requirement to address intermittency", said Ivan.

"I looked at battery storage as one option", Meg started, only for Ivan to interrupt her.

"Batteries are great but would not be an ideal option for long-term utility scale solutions. If a major city like London or Tokyo goes down for a few days, batteries will not be able to bridge that gap", Ivan said.

"There is pumped hydro, essentially something similar to your dams where you pump the water up when you have surplus energy and drop the water through turbines when your power supply is off. This is efficient and has been around for a long time and can be looked at as a large utility-scale energy storage solution, but the issue is you cannot have it everywhere. The geography has to support it with elevation and water supply, preferably rivers on mountains.

Then there is what we call liquid air where we compress air at high pressures, convert it to liquid and store it in tanks. When necessary, we can release this liquid air, heat it up and run it through turbines to generate electricity. This is a proven technology and has been around for a while and can be looked at as a mid-range energy storage solution.

And then there is the option of using the surplus energy to generate hydrogen through electrolysis, store the hydrogen in the distribution network or in salt caverns and use the hydrogen to generate electricity either through fuel cells or through other means like combined cycle gas turbines.

Whichever option you take, and they all have their advantages and disadvantages in terms of technology, efficiencies and so on, you will need an equivalent capacity of storage and regeneration capacity.

If you are replacing a coal-fired power station of one-megawatt capacity, with a combination of intermittent renewables, say solar and wind, you will still need a storage and regeneration unit of one-megawatt capacity, be it hydro or liquid air or hydrogen based or a combination of these, to supply the city when solar and wind power go silent".

Meg remained silent for a moment and said, "Are we saying that we may require up to seven times the capacity to replace an existing power plant with renewables?"

Ivan said, "Well, it is more like four to five times for solar replacements and if we have a combination of solar and wind, the intermittency reduces further. Keep in mind that building a coal-fired power station can be about three to four times the cost of putting up a solar facility for the same capacity.

And the most important thing is we have not included the cost of carbon capture for the coal-fired power station. We need to compare apples for apples. If the carbon dioxide is captured at the coal-fired power station, that too becomes clean but the upfront capital cost to build it will be much higher than the renewable options".

Meg sighed in relief.

Ivan continued, "And your cost per unit calculations will still be valid for the solar farms as you have only considered four hours of production per day. With the money you get for the energy, the feed-in-tariff, the cost estimates for operating the solar farm should stack up. The only outstanding item will be the capital cost of the storage and regeneration facility.

I think, from the technical perspective, we should be able to put a proposal together. It will not be just solar but a combination of multiple technologies. Similarly, the package to store the energy and regenerate on demand will be a combination of battery, liquid air, hydrogen and pumped hydro, as an example.

I will get my team to run some real numbers on all these options. We will do some preliminary work on this and paint a picture".

Meg thanked Ivan and took leave.

CHAPTER 14

Job Transition

"What are we looking at?" asked Claire, the Secretary of Innovation, Training and Education, as Meg and Palucci entered her office and made themselves comfortable.

"There is the issue of job losses", Meg began speaking, "All FrICE projects are designed to eliminate labour. Full automation is part of the design which means job losses will occur in those sectors. Eventually, we will have no people working in agriculture or in manufacturing. Both sectors will become people free.

Globally, billions of people are engaged in both the sectors. Many people working in the agricultural sector are landowners working on their own land. However, a lot of casual labour is also involved in this sector. With the advent of full automation, all these people will be impacted.

We need a clear method and solution on how we are going to manage this transition; how we are going to steer and guide the people through this job loss scenario. I have some ideas in this space, but it certainly needs to be discussed and validated".

"Okay. Let us hear it", said Claire.

"We propose that any worker in an impacted industry needs to be supported in the transition. FrICE projects will need to contribute to this transition fund for impacted people in their industry. This contribution needs to be taken into account as a cost in the debt-repayment model".

"But what is the transition strategy. Are we going to support everyone? Are there any eligibility criteria for this transition support?" asked Claire.

Palucci said, "Let us put some criteria in place and then we can discuss that. Let us say a person should have worked in an industry for the last ten years, as a minimum, to be considered an eligible candidate for transition support. The logic is, if the person has been working in other sectors in the last ten years, then they will find it easier to transition to those sectors, with minimal support".

"Sounds okay", said Claire, "Now, for those eligible, are we going to support them with a basic wage for the rest of their life? Are we going to train them to gain new skills and move them on to different sectors? What is the plan?"

"We will need different strategies for different

conditions. Retraining is okay, but I do not think it is for everyone. Say someone who has been an underground coal miner for most of their life, with another five years to retirement, may not be the best candidate to be retrained as a computer programmer", said Meg.

"Why not? I might know of someone who might fit the bill", Claire teased Meg.

"Well, you know what I mean. Retraining is good only when other factors are considered as well. The age of the candidate will matter. Alignment of the new skill will matter. It is easier to retrain a fitter to be a welder than to be a bookkeeper. I am not saying it is not possible, just that this may require more effort to make the jump. I think the interest and willingness of the candidate is also a very important factor to be considered, probably the primary factor", said Meg.

Claire said, "Looks like we will offer retraining to people considering their interest and willingness to be retrained, the age factor and of course the skillset alignment factor. So, let us look at some practical examples. Consider a young person, who is single and with minimal family commitments, who has been working in a coal-powered power generation plant for ten years. What is the exit plan for this person?"

Meg replied, "First, people need a clear indication that the particular industry will be impacted by FrICE and there will be job losses. As an example, all companies in the coal industry need to let their current employees, and any new recruits, know that the company will cease to operate in say ten years' time. This way people have time to digest the upcoming change, plan for it and transition accordingly.

For this younger person, I think there will be general agreement that retraining will be the preferred strategy. The person will be clearly told that this sector will be shutting down in the coming years and that they will need to get on a retraining programme that they think will suit them best. They will then kick off the process with a transition counsellor, pick areas of interest to move on and start retraining. Let us say the retraining process takes three to four years to effectively position the young employee in another viable sector".

"And who is going to pay for the retraining?" asked Claire.

"FrICE will fund the retraining from the money they have put aside for the impacted people", said Meg.

"Okay. Let us look at another example. Consider a middle-aged person, say someone in their forties, married with three kids, who has been in the sector for around twenty years working in the same coal-powered power generation plant. What is the exit plan for this person?" asked Claire.

"For the middle-aged person, retraining must be seriously considered and would be a similar process to the younger person", replied Palucci.

"Is there going to be any financial support during this transition and retraining period, where they might be between jobs?"

"If they are given sufficient advance notice, say ten years, as we discussed earlier, it is highly unlikely that they wouldn't have transitioned yet. And in cases where they haven't and are between jobs, how about if FrICE were to pay the basic minimum wage for a period of five years after the mine closure", said Meg.

"Okay. How about a senior person who has been in the sector for all of their working life with just a few more years to their retirement? What do we do in their case?"

Palucci responded, "In that situation, providing them with a basic minimum wage till they reach pensionable age might be the best option for all concerned. If retraining and redeployment takes a few years, the person has only a very limited time engaging in effective work in the new sector. Now, if they want to continue to work and want to get retrained, sure, we should offer them that. But otherwise, providing them with a basic minimum wage would be a better option, in my opinion".

Meg continued on that point, "Let us peg an age, say when social security kicks in, and let us work back from that. How about if FrICE were to pay a basic minimum wage for all people who are within ten years of availing social security or reaching pensionable age? That way they are financially sustained till social security or pension kicks in".

Claire said, "One thing that seems to stand out is that the older a person is, the longer it takes them to learn new skills and successfully transition to a new industry. If that is the case, why don't we scale the support accordingly. If we were to say that we provide four years of basic minimum wage for anyone under forty years of age and increase the support period by two years for each additional ten years in age".

"So, anyone over forty gets six years, over fifty gets eight years and over sixty get ten years of basic minimum wage support. Sounds good. However, I have a concern. This basic minimum wage might be okay for a single person. But would that be sufficient for a family to live on?" asked Meg.

Claire responded, "Let us look at it this way. Currently there are programmes run by social services that provide unemployment benefits, retraining and job-seeking support. Strictly speaking, we can continue with that financial support. From what I am hearing, it feels like people impacted by FrICE are to be treated different and are going to get better support. Should that be the case?"

"If we are talking equitable support, it is probably not the right thing to do. But the current social security support is barely scratching the surface for most people who are jobless. FrICE will add more numbers to that group. We just want to make sure that people do not go anti-FrICE because of this. We want them to welcome FrICE and support it. Otherwise, the concept will not fly. So, it is probably not a bad idea to add additional support payments for people impacted by FrICE", said Meg.

Palucci said, "We are looking at the slingshot strategy, leaping over the impending dominance of AI and massive job losses. FrICE is our answer. I think we need to promote it and paint a positive picture".

"What about parts of the world where there is no social security blanket for their people?" asked Claire.

"Well, in that case, the FrICE payment will be seen as a positive, wouldn't it? As a minimum, people will be getting some financial support from FrICE compared to other job loss events", replied Meg.

Claire summarized the discussion saying, "Okay, then it is agreed that all FrICE-impacted people, in terms of job loss, will get additional compensation from FrICE, over and above what they will be getting from social services.

The impacted person needs to have been working in that particular sector for a minimum period of time to be eligible for this additional FrICE benefit.

The eligible, impacted person will be provided with basic minimum wage transition support for a period of time, between four and ten years, indexed to their age. The eligible person is also provided with necessary education, skills and training during this transition phase, for a successful transition to the new industry, as required".

CHAPTER 15

Education

"I have another question. We have implemented FrICE and everything is for free for everyone. The utopian dream has been realized. Now what? What are people going to do? More to the point, why should anybody do anything when everything is for free?" asked Claire.

Meg replied, "Very valid question. Currently most of the people are wasting their time and effort on mechanical, repetitive tasks as part of their jobs".

"Are we talking of factory workers?"

"We are not limiting ourselves to that. Most jobs do not need any fresh thinking or creativity. Take an accountant. At a basic level, they can be replaced by software which means all that they do is to follow a set of rules and apply those accounting rules to classify the financial numbers. Strictly speaking, there is no creative work here – nothing new".

"Well, strictly speaking you do not want any

creative work in that space", Claire smiled.

"You know what I mean", said Meg, "You can take many other jobs and they would all be mundane, repetitive tasks that follow a protocol, a set of rules, and a machine can replace those people. Even so-called professional jobs like doctors and lawyers, at the basic level, can be added to this category".

"I get it, carry on", said Claire.

"With FrICE, all of these jobs will be gone, replaced by machines. All the people who were pulling levers are now jobless and they are free, with pretty much nothing to do. We potentially have seven billion heads that can be trained to do creative work. Now is the opportunity for people to think different, get creative and propose innovative solutions to the next generation of needs, wants and quests.

With FrICE, we will have a global population with a lot of 'free' time in their hands. We will also have a population that needs to be educated, to be trained for a range of skills that we will need in the future".

"What are these skills that we are going to need in the future? With everything for free, what are going to be our new needs?" asked Claire.

Palucci stepped in and said, "The answer is, we don't know. But what we know for sure is that they will evolve. If history is any indication, we will always surprise ourselves with new inventions and innovations, and an educated population enhances our potential to invent and innovate".

Meg continued, "So, the plan is as follows. All individuals register with FrICE to engage with and benefit from the free everything provision. In turn, individuals covenant that they will continue their education, completing at least one unit of learning every six months, as long as they are not effectively engaged in other social contributory activities like a job, volunteering and so on. The cumulative units will be spread across at least three different streams.

This way people gain the necessary education, skills and training to actively contribute in the new economy. It also gives people some structure and discipline, if needed".

"Interesting", said Claire. "Are we talking of everyone going to college? Is there an age limit? When do they stop educating themselves?"

"We are looking at promoting education for life", responded Meg.

"For life? Really? Is that necessary?"

"Well, how about we ensure that people continue to educate themselves, till they are ten years from what is considered to be the average lifespan of humans, at that point in time".

"Why ten years? Why don't we let the medical experts nominate an age beyond which the mental capability of humans is not conducive for learning new stuff?"

"We can go look at that. In the absence of any other structured activity for that semester, this educational requirement will keep people engaged. And education will certainly improve the awareness of people, improve the quality of our citizenry".

"Okay. Do you think getting people to do one unit of study per semester is going to improve the quality of our citizenry?"

"Yes and no. We have some critical issues with our educational system that need to be addressed and resolved. Once we have done that, this ongoing education will certainly deliver. I believe that we should take this opportunity and blend in this change to our educational curriculum as part of the FrICE initiative".

"What changes are you proposing?"

"Our current education system is classroom focused. It prepares students to engage in a 19th-century industrial economy. Students are 'taught', and they 'repeat' the information through 'exams'. The system trains students to function in a pyramid power structure, taking orders and doing the task. Collaborative effort is punished as 'copying'".

Claire smiled at the last comment.

"With FrICE, we will have seven billion heads

freed up, available to explore the problem of the day and arrive at creative solutions. Collaborative innovation will be the need of the day. The new system should promote confluence of seemingly unrelated interdisciplinary combinations that are the wellspring of innovation".

Claire raised her hand and gently brought Meg to a halt. She said, "That is a lot of words and a lot of passion. It is all great but what are we going to do that is different?"

"First let us question the current educational system in terms of the period of education. We have around twelve years of schooling and an additional three to four years of college education which is optional. Why do we limit ourselves to less than twenty years of education, on average? Wouldn't more skills, knowledge and training be better for everyone?

Most of the current graduates then enter the workforce and engage in what is considered to be a productive career. In most cases, people are just prepped up to join the conga line and keep pulling levers.

FrICE will not limit education in this basis. Under FrICE, education will continue on, as we discussed earlier. FrICE will not specify what people need to study as part of this ongoing education but will promote people completing units in varied streams".

"And why would that be?" asked Claire.

"Multi-stream knowledge will be a key initiator for innovative solutions. Typically, innovation brings together two seemingly disparate aspects to create a new concept, method, system or process that benefits humans. Combining the use of lasers in medical procedures revolutionized corrective eye surgery. Combining the smartphone capability with apps and taxi business model, the rideshare industry has evolved.

For us to tap into this stream of innovative solutions, we need people educated and trained in disparate streams to be aware of and identify these potential solutions.

The other requirement for a multi-faceted education is to address the fact that just about all issues and solutions in real life are multi-dimensional. If one proposes building a dam as a pumped hydro solution for clean renewable energy storage, the people who are involved in these decisions need to look at the proposed solution from a technical, financial, political, economic, ethical and environmental perspective, to name just a few. Depending on where the proposed dam is going to be located, geological and seismic studies may become relevant in terms of assessing the suitability of the site. Or linguistics and anthropology may be relevant to assess the impact of the dam on the local tribal population.

A person engaged in a project like this need not be an expert in every aspect, but an awareness and understanding of these aspects will certainly help in effective decision making and delivering quality solutions.

The new education system will also need to have the flexibility to cater to specific tailored market requirements. As an example, the market may need archaeologists specializing in Egyptian ruins, with expertise in hieroglyphs and radiology. The flexible system should be able to deliver either a vertically integrated or a lateral spread of knowledge as may be the requirement of that time", said Meg.

"Sounds good", said Claire, "So, we are going to have people on an ongoing education stream, doing a unit every semester, learning new knowledge and skills, in multiple streams, till a nominated age. Now the question is, who is going to pay for this ongoing education?"

"I have been thinking about this", said Meg, "Even today, with college education, most of the lectures are online. Tutorials are conducted by senior students. If we look at a virtual university, we may be able to deliver education cost free".

"So, what happens to classes, lectures, tutorials and so on?"

"There will be no in-person classes or lectures. We will deliver courses online. We will conduct tutorials using senior students. And with that we probably do not need real estate as well".

"And the senior students will deliver it for free?"

"Why not? I believe that the best way to ensure thorough understanding of a subject matter is to try and teach it to someone. It doesn't take long to realize how shaky your grasp on the concept is", said Meg with a smile that indicated personal experience and continued, "I think it will work if we make it a part of their course and give them credit points for that?"

"Debatable, but let's go on. What about assessments, exams, certification?"

"Once again, we can use technology to conduct assessments and examinations to a large extent".

"To a certain extent, yes. But there are going to be some scenarios where this may not be possible. However, a more important issue is the development of the young person in university. University is not just about learning the subject matter. There is social interaction, guidance, mentoring and so on that forms a part of the young person's overall development", said Claire.

"True. But we are not necessarily talking of young people. We are talking of most of the adult population going through some ongoing education. The young people, fifteen to twenty-five years of age, constitute only about 17% of the world population. The adults aged twenty-five plus make up over 65% of the world population.

With most of this adult population engaging in this ongoing education, the universities will be predominantly catering to this subset of the population. And typically, the adult population will not need guidance and mentoring in terms of their development as much as the young people.

As such, we can have two different streams of education. We can have one for the adults addressing ongoing education, predominantly focused on the subject matter with a low level of interpersonal guidance, mentoring and engagement. This way, we can significantly reduce the cost of the ongoing adult education programme. For the young people, we can continue with the current model", responded Meg.

"I like the two-pronged approach. That will certainly help with optimizing education cost", said Claire and continued, "however, what about content? Use of books and course material? There will be a payment to the content generators".

Meg thought for a while and said, "True. And we don't want our content to be IP expired and outdated. We will want the latest and the best. So, we will need to spend on paying for content. There is going to be some cost for the course content and that will apply for both streams. Further, we just agreed that we will not eliminate human interaction completely. We will need lecturers and professors to engage with and mentor young students to deliver real value".

"Why don't we get George in this conversation. He may have some thoughts on this", said Claire.

"Sounds great", said Meg. "Can you bring him in?"

Claire did. George listened to the scenario of making education cost free.

"Let us go through this", he said. "Currently the government funds part of the education. The rest is covered by student loan that is interest free and the student only has to repay it once they hit a certain level of salary. Correct?"

"Yes".

"Why don't we continue the same system? As per your logic, the cost of education will significantly reduce due to technology. For ongoing adult education, it will be even lower as we are going to have minimal in-person guidance and mentoring.

We expect people to benefit from this education and in turn generate creative things that will benefit humanity. The creators can then charge for these creative things when they are still in their IP period and pay back their education loans".

"I agree", said Claire. "Under FrICE, especially

with the education focus that we are implementing, it is very likely that a whole new range of things are going to be invented and innovated. It is going to be a whole new economy, much bigger to our current economy, even when we exclude agriculture and manufacturing, going forward".

"So, are we saying that the students will be able to sell their creation in the market and they can pay off their student loan from the proceeds?" asked Meg.

"It is either that or we tax the new creations on their proceeds and pay off the student loans in a collective approach", said George.

CHAPTER 16

Round Table – How FrICE Works

When all participants were settled in, Palucci kicked off the session saying, "Thanks for coming everyone. Initially we thought it would be a good idea to meet with each and every one of you individually and discuss specific aspects of this project in further detail. We kicked it off with some sectors with good results. We were able to resolve some of the technical aspects with ease. However, a range of other issues needed consultation with multiple departments. Hence, we thought it would be a better option to convene everyone together for a few short sessions and have this conversation".

Claire said, "I think that is not a bad idea. Instead of vacillating, it gives the opportunity to discuss the various facets of this project in a single conversation".

Palucci nodded in acknowledgement and asked Meg to kick off the meeting.

Meg said, "Once again, thanks for coming. By

adopting FrICE, we have a range of associated issues that we will need to discuss and agree upon. First item I would like to table is the issue of using clean, renewable energy going forward. We will not be using fossil fuels as part of the solution. Is that doable?"

Ivan said, "Yes and no. Yes, the market is expecting us to go that way. Big investment banks have been moving away from coal, for sure. It is very difficult to get a proposal approved for a coal-based power generation plant today. Natural gas is a different beast though. There is political will and commitment to natural gas.

Our political and energy leadership view the clean renewables like solar and wind with some concern, predominantly due to their intermittency and ability to provide utility-scale solutions. They are risk averse and see natural gas as the solution today, even if the market is not very favourable on that. The industry lobby has its role in this decision as well".

"However, I do not think this is a bad situation to be in", Ivan looked at Meg and said, "FrICE does not necessarily require clean renewable energy; it just needs free energy. FrICE model can work with free energy from any source. Correct?"

Meg nodded in agreement.

"Good. Then, the only reason we want to go the clean renewable way is because of climate change issues. On the other hand, if the government of the day is going with natural gas as the solution, that is not a bad outcome for FrICE. The government will gradually replace coal-based power generation with natural gas–based power generation. Once FrICE sets up the clean renewable power generation facilities like solar and wind, we can use the excess power to make hydrogen and use this hydrogen as feedstock for our baseload power generation. We can store this hydrogen in the natural gas piping system or in salt caverns. We can infuse this hydrogen into the natural gas system thus reducing our carbon emission. When we have enough hydrogen, we can slightly modify the natural gas power generators to run on hydrogen, thus making a complete transition to clean renewable energy".

Ivan turned to Meg and said, "Remember how we discussed the power generation capacity we will need for storage and regeneration? This way we can use this natural gas infrastructure to address the issue of energy storage and regeneration that we will have to deal with for any intermittent energy source. As discussed, we could generate hydrogen from surplus energy, store it in the gas network as well as salt caverns and use that as fuel in the natural gas power generators".

"So, what do we need to do now to limit the impact

of this transition from natural gas to hydrogen? There are people putting their money in natural gas infrastructure development today and we do not want them to be unnecessarily impacted", said Palucci.

"There are two parts to it. One is the natural gas production, wells and other facilities that extract the natural gas from below. The other is the power generation facility that uses the natural gas to generate electricity.

We need to specify that the power generation facility being built today has to be able to run on multiple fuels including hydrogen. When free hydrogen economy kicks in, the natural gas requirement will be replaced by hydrogen. Our natural gas production facilities will become redundant. So, we are better off buying our natural gas instead of developing our own natural gas production facilities in the transition period. That way, when we switch to hydrogen, we can walk away clean and no one gets financially hurt", said Ivan.

Claire asked, "I need some clarification on this. How do transactions happen in FrICE?"

Meg said, "Any organization or individual that wishes to participate in FrICE transactions will need to engage in a FrICE contract and be registered as part of FrICE. When an organization registers with FrICE, it covenants to receive free inputs from FrICE organizations upstream. It will add value to the free inputs and deliver the output for free to downstream FrICE-registered organizations or individual end users. For items that are not consumed, the end user, be it an individual or an organization, in turn, is contractually obliged to return the unconsumed part of the product for recycling, at end-of-life replacement".

Meg continued, "Let us consider a FrICE-registered organization that runs a factory or mine or farm. Our organization can receive, for free, all machines required to build or refurbish their fully automated factory or mine or farm from FrICE Shuru factories. Further, it can receive, for free, the services of FrICE construction companies that assemble the machines and build the factory or mine or farm for free. Thus, capital cost is eliminated for our FrICE-registered organization".

"With a fully automated factory or mine or farm, no labour is required. Hence, labour cost is eliminated.

Our organization can receive energy and all raw materials from other FrICE organizations upstream, for free, to run the factory or mine or farm. With energy, raw material, labour and capital costs eliminated, the organization can now produce the output for free".

"Okay. How do these transactions between organizations work? How will we track the material movement? How do we track who gives what to whom? How will we know who has possession of that material at any point in time?" asked Claire.

"We use block chain technology to track material movement", said Meg. "All these transactions will be captured in block chain registers for tracking and compliance.

As a FrICE member, let us say you go to the manufacturing pod, tap your FrICE card and get an aluminium water bottle for free. When the water bottle is manufactured by the pod, it carries an embedded microchip ID and is tagged as something that needs to be recycled. The water bottle may have a use-by or expiry or return-by date assigned to it, if appropriate.

Robots read the embedded microchip ID and record the movement of the water bottle. When you get the water bottle, the embedded microchip records the transaction, in block chain registers, that the bottle has moved to your possession and the block chain ledger is updated accordingly. Now you carry the water bottle on your block chain account.

When you return the bottle for recycling, the bottle is sent to your local waste processing facility. The embedded microchip indicates to the block chain that the material has been sent for recycling. The bottle has moved from your possession to the recycling facility and the block chain ledger is updated accordingly.

Let us look at a slightly more complex transaction, the lifecycle of a fridge. A fridge is made of many components. Let us track one of them, its compressor. The compressor is made in factories using components that are predominantly made of metals such as steel and copper.

Working back, let us say iron ore and copper ore is provided by the respective mines to steel- and copper-making factories, for free. This transaction is captured in block chain registers indicating transfer of custodianship of the ore material from the mine to the metal factories.

For fungible, bulk commodities like ore, information such as weight or volume of the commodity transferred, and the material specification, is captured as part of the transaction in block chain registers.

The metal factories make steel and copper respectively from the free ore. They then transfer the metal, for free, to Shuru factories that make compressors. This transaction is also captured in block chain registers similar to the ore transaction.

The Shuru factories will now use the free metals to make compressors. Each compressor, and its components, that is manufactured at this Shuru factory will be assigned a unique identification and have this ID embedded in them.

The embedded ID will hold the ancestral

information on this compressor; information on the ore such as the mine and the batch, information on the metal such as the factory and the amount of each raw material used to make this compressor.

It will also hold information on the recycle protocol of this compressor including procedure to dismantle the compressor, segregation of its components and specifying the recycling process for each component. This embedded information will enable us to track this compressor through its life cycle and facilitate the return of the raw material to the source, if so required".

"So, how does this embedded ID work?"

"Well, we can look at it as a bar code or QR code or an embedded microchip in that component that holds all the information on the component. The compressor and its sub-components will individually have embedded microchips that will hold the information including things like where it was made and when, the type of material and specification, the energy expended in making that component and its recycling protocol that specifies the recycling method, process and information on other materials it can mix with during recycling, as a minimum.

Robotic readers capture this embedded ID information as the component changes hands and the transaction is automatically recorded, with all the associated information, in block chain registers.

Now coming back to our transaction, the compressor in turn will be given to other FrICE-registered Shuru factories that use it to make other machine assemblies such as air conditioners, fridges or freezers. Robotic readers will capture this embedded ID information and record this transaction in block chain registers.

Let us follow our compressor that becomes a part of the fridge. The fridge manufacturer will use the compressor to build the fridge. The fridge in turn is assigned a unique identification and all information on it and its sub-components, including the compressor, is embedded in the fridge, in the form of a microchip.

Now the fridge changes hands and is provided to an end user for free. This transfer is recorded in block chain registers. The custodianship of the fridge, its sub-components and the material used to manufacture the components, gets transferred to the end user this point onwards till he or she disposes off the fridge. Block chain tracks and assigns the material debt to the end user, factoring in the material loss over its life. The material debt stays with the end user for the estimated life of the asset and is reset on recycling", said Meg.

"So, how does recycling work under FrICE?" asked Claire.

"Let us say the fridge has an estimated life of ten years. When our fridge reaches end of its life and the user wants to replace it with another free fridge, they return the old one to a recycling facility.

Robots at the recycling facility dismantle the fridge and read the microchipped information in the fridge and its individual components. The robots send each component on its recycling path depending on its recycling protocol, as read from the embedded chip".

"What if I do not recycle the fridge and keep getting new fridges?" asked Claire.

"Well, then all of the material debt will be staying in your FrICE account", said Meg.

"And is there a penalty for that? Do I have to pay a fine or go to jail?"

Palucci stepped in and said, "Let us understand this. Under FrICE, clean energy is abundant and free. So, that is not a key driver for recycling. The key issues for recycling are material pollution due to synthetics and the issue of finite resources. We are all well aware of the pollution issue on our hands due to the usage of non-biodegradable plastics. We need to recycle plastics and that is a given.

Metal deposits are also finite, limited and eminently recyclable. It makes much better sense to take used steel and bring it back to life instead of digging fresh ore, which may potentially run out, and going through the whole process to make fresh steel takes a lot more time and energy.

It would be irresponsible for us, as a society, to not recycle material, where possible. We have not proposed any punitive measures for not clearing your material debt. Society can always do that – could be a fine or community service, or correctional service. The importance of recycling is something to be decided by the society. What we propose is the method to recycle. How well we enforce them is for society to decide".

"That sounds fair", said Claire, "by the way, earlier you mentioned recycling the unconsumed part. What was that about?"

Meg replied, "Well, when you get a fridge, most of the fridge is there to be returned at the end of ten years. If the fridge weighed a hundred kilos when you took delivery of it, it most likely will weigh the same when you send it for recycling.

However, the story is different when you get a free ice cream. You may tap your FrICE ID card and get a free ice cream. Block chain transactions will have assigned the ice cream and the cup against your FrICE account. By design, the ice cream will not remain in your FrICE account as it is to be consumed. However, the cup will remain in your FrICE account, if it is recyclable. You may drop the cup in recycling bins where readers will capture the transaction and your FrICE account will be cleared of the cup".

"Interesting", said Claire, "It sounds similar to a lending library setup. You register as a member of your local council library to borrow books. Both you and the library have a record of this borrowing. You need to return the book in a stipulated timeframe. You can return it earlier and borrow another book. If you don't return the book, you incur a fine which may equate to the value of the book and more".

Palucci commented, "That is a neat comparison. Just that, currently only the library has the records. Under a block chain system, the transactions are secure and will be set in stone, so to speak. With multiple copies of the same transaction across the globe, it will be extremely difficult to modify or delete agreed transactions".

The group broke up for the day with Palucci organizing for another session the next week.

CHAPTER 17

Round Table — Money and Metrics

Ivan opened the session with a question, "If everything is free, is there no more money involved in transactions in the future?"

George, the Treasury Secretary, said, "Let us think this through. What happens when things become free? Use of money will reduce. Progressively we will have more and more FrICE transactions happening with no money transfer. For instance, you may have FrICE sugar and regular sugar available in the market. The FrICE sugar will be free and the regular sugar will be sold at the market price. As FrICE sugar production picks up, we are going to have more free sugar available to meet the global demand. At this point, people will stop paying for sugar and commercial Sugar Mills will close as it will not be sustainable to produce sugar at a cost and sell it for less than cost".

"So, during this transition, we will still be using money, correct?"

George responded, "I think we will continue to use money, just that there will be less in circulation. Progressively, use of money for material things will cease as FrICE becomes prevalent in the future.

And correct me if I am wrong, not everything is going to be free. Only material things. New ideas and creations will still be charged for. People's time can still be charged for, if they are delivering value. So, yes, I think we will still have a system to peg value and enable transactions".

Meg added, "For example, someone may bring out a new flavoured ice cream and may put a monetary price on it. If the consumer finds it to be good enough, they will pay the asking price. If not, the ice cream is given away for free".

Palucci said, "I think mediums of exchange other than money will come in to use".

"Really, like what?" asked Claire.

Palucci replied, "Well, I recently saw a celebrity mention that she paid for some hair styling work with an Instagram post. I think social media engagement points will be a critical medium of exchange, going forward; we could even call them SMEPs.

Consider the ice cream example. If I were to create the new ice cream, I could sell it for say a few dollars. Or I could offer it in exchange for a few social media engagement points such as likes, comments, shares, subscribes, followers and so on".

"Interesting point. I can see the shift towards what you call SMEPs", said Claire.

"If my ice cream is good enough that a million people are willing to SMEP it, my social footprint is enhanced".

"And what are you going to do with an enhanced social footprint?"

"I don't know. I might become a member of the million SMEP club. I might get preference in queues to shows, concerts or even boarding a plane. My influence quotient may increase. I potentially have a platform with a million people that I can possibly communicate with. Even today, while material wealth enables us to get things, a social or celebrity quotient is much more impactful in influencing outcomes".

"I agree", said George, "maybe that is where things will go. Maybe SMEPs will be a player in transactions in the future. However, it opens up a very interesting scenario. The transaction is not for free. You, as the creator of the ice cream, are benefitting from the consumer. Just not in dollars but in SMEPs. So how do we tax you on that?"

Palucci let out a hearty laugh and said, "George, go figure that out".

Ivan continued, "Coming back to the use of money, we may not be using money for getting a fridge or a pound of sugar, but we might still be paying money to watch a play or a musical performance. FrICE only makes material things free, not creative content.

And how many pounds of sugar will you take for one balcony ticket?"

"Why would I trade my ticket for sugar when I also get sugar for free? So strictly speaking, there is no monetary value on sugar. It is freely available for everyone", said Palucci.

Claire said, "If everything is free, how do we know the value of any item?"

"But why do you need to assign a value on something?" asked Ivan.

Meg responded, "Maybe when you want to swap something for another thing?"

"Are we down to barter?" asked Claire.

Palucci stepped in and said, "Look, Meg and I discussed this. One of the options we have considered is the embedded energy value or the e'value. Since everything is energy based, we can have a new accounting system for any material thing based on the amount of energy that went into making it.

As an example, one kg of steel will have an e'value that is the pro-rata energy required to produce it, which will be an amalgamation of the energy required to extract the ore, smelt the ore and make the metal.

A compressor will have the e'value of the metals

and plastic that has gone into it as raw materials. We also need to add the proportional energy used in manufacturing the compressor in the Shuru factory. This will be the equivalent of our operational cost value.

Let us not forget the equivalent of capital cost assignment. We also need to add the proportional energy value of the Shuru factory – the e'value of raw materials and the energy that went in to making the factory. So, if the Shuru factory is designed to produce a million compressors, each compressor carries one millionth of the Shuru factory's e'value".

Ivan responded, "I think e'value may not provide the correct picture. Based on the e'value system, a FrICE bread maker could produce a loaf of bread for say a hundred e'values, while another produces the same loaf of bread for a thousand e'values. Does it mean the second one is ten times more productive? It is just that the second bread maker is not using energy in an efficient manner".

Palucci said, "Okay, how about if we add an adjustment factor for efficiency. We pick the e'value of the most efficient bread made, at hundred e'values and assign it as a nominal e'value to all bread".

Meg responded, "Or we could take the average e'value of all bread made and use that as the metric".

George commented, "From an accounting

perspective, we can treat this system like a value-added taxation system. Let us get this clear. The e'value provides an indication of the actual energy input. With the efficiency factor, we will have an adjusted value that might be a better indication of nominal energy input for that product. However, the beauty of our current system is that the price incorporates both the inputs and what the consumer is willing to pay. With e'value, the consumer side of the equation is completely missing".

Palucci responded, "Well, the e'value does not replace the price. For any free transaction, no price is required. The consumer side of the equation is addressed by the demand for that item.

For the ice cream that we discussed earlier, Claire might fix a price for the ice cream based on either dollars or SMEPs. If the consumer thinks it is worth it, they pay. If they do not, we have no sale and Claire will need to drop her price or close shop. So, the market system still works, just that it does not come into play for any free transaction".

The discussion turned to economic metrics.

George said, "Let us keep in mind that we created metrics like the GDP (gross domestic product) to track the health of our economy in the current model. Under FrICE, I think we are going to need a new set of metrics to do the same.

The GDP is the total monetary value of all the finished goods and services produced. GDP under FrICE will not truly reflect the state of our economy. Under FrICE, when we produce more, our GDP may show that our economy is shrinking because the metric measures money, and there is diminished or no money transaction to reflect the material transaction".

Ivan responded, "So, measuring money is out. How about measuring nominal, efficiency adjusted, e'value as an economic metric. This can possibly represent our economic health and replace GDP. In effect, all we are doing is tracking the energy that we produce, store and consume. Is that right?"

George said, "It could be one of the metrics that we start tracking in the new world. However, as I mentioned earlier, we need to keep in mind that FrICE brings about a new way of doing things and we will need new metrics, new ways of measuring our economic performance".

Meg said, "On another front, typically, our energy consumption indicates our standard of living. So, this will be a pretty good metric to indicate where we are in the scheme of things.

One of the social aspects we want to address through FrICE is to address global poverty. Currently we define poverty with a monetary metric, pegged at $2.00 per person per day. With the emergence of e'values, we should take this opportunity to redefine it based on energy consumed. We are proposing a new global poverty metric of 1 Kw per capita".

Claire said, "Wow, wouldn't that be way off the current measure?"

"Yes, and it is time to redefine poverty", said Meg. "All this while we have been sticking to the two-dollar mark and we have showed significant progress, mostly from China in the last few decades. However, with FrICE, we have the ability to generate vast amounts of usable energy; we can eliminate poverty and inequality related to material things.

Currently the population in developed countries consumes this amount of energy per capita. People in developed countries enjoy this level of living standard. It is time for us to bring the rest of the global population to the same level. Let us redefine poverty as not less than 1 kilowatt of power generation capacity per capita".

Ivan said, "I think it is a good idea. We are looking at a huge global change. We need to think big, redefine our benchmarks and set them high".

Meg turned to George and said, "I wanted some clarification on one critical aspect. If the flow of money diminishes, what is the impact on the finance industry?"

"Yes. What happens to the stock market? Will the

banks still be in business?" asked Claire.

George said, "I have been thinking about this. If we are successful with FrICE, the so-called traditional businesses, those that have agriculture or mining or manufacturing as their core activity, will cease to function in a commercial manner over a period of time. That part of the stock market may be impacted".

"Are we saying that the Dow Jones will cease to exist and only the Nasdaq will survive?"

George responded, "Only to a certain extent. I agree that in the recent past, the software industry has had more new ideas and content compared to a traditional rice mill or a bread factory. However, I think any business that creates new value, in terms of new ideas and new content, will survive as commercial entities".

Meg said, "One of the pillars of FrICE is innovation. In its essence, FrICE promotes people and companies coming up with new ideas. FrICE makes it easier to take the idea to the market.

The only covenant is that under FrICE, all new innovations are subject to intellectual property laws and will have an expiry date. The company, or person, can enjoy rights to the innovation and make money off it for the stipulated period upon which the innovation transfers to the public domain".

Palucci said, "As long as businesses are innovating

and bringing new ideas and content, they will survive under the commercial model. I think the financial industry will follow the innovative, successful businesses".

Claire said, "I think banks and financial lending may bite the dust under FrICE. If I need a new factory to manufacture my new idea, I do not need to go to a bank and ask for money to build the factory; FrICE will build the factory for free. So why do I need a bank or a lending institution?"

George concluded the discussion saying, "I think it would be safe to say that the financial industry's profile and influence on economic activity will be diminished post FrICE, unless they get innovative and start dealing with and managing other mediums of exchange as well".

Meg asked, "George, are you comfortable with the numbers we have crunched to justify FrICE projects?"

"I don't think we have even scratched the surface yet", said George and continued, "But, I think it is a good approach that you have adopted in funding FrICE projects. I like the idea of public participation in promoting these projects. That way you design a commercially attractive project that appeals to the public. With popular public support, you will have sufficient political support as well and that will certainly minimize roadblocks for these projects".

"But the most important point from his perspective is that you are not coming to Treasury asking to fund the whole project", smiled Claire.

"Absolutely correct", said George, "and even if you did, we may not be able to fund the initiative unless we take on a high level of debt and that would bring its own political issues. But under the proposed model, I think we can facilitate the process and support it with some leverage funding".

Looking at Meg's puzzled look, George explained, "The government supports many industries with subsidies. Energy sector, the farming sector and health care sector are some of the biggest recipients of government subsidies. The subsidies take various forms such as tax breaks, cash incentives, loans and guarantees at favourable rates, price controls, providing resources like land and water for free or at below-market rates, research and development funding; it is a long list.

I see that you have assumed some of these subsidies for your FrICE projects already, like free government land for the solar farms".

Ivan stepped in and said, "The government subsidizes traditional energy sector. It is interesting to note that without these subsidies, traditional energy is more expensive than renewable energy, as of today. And due to these subsidies, the renewable energy sector struggles to compete against the traditional sector to secure funding".

"True", said George. "In principle, I am against subsidies. They distort the market. The market only sees a discounted price, not the real price. However, I think I will support subsidies for FrICE for a couple of reasons.

The first is that the FrICE projects are designed to be financially self-sufficient. People lend to cover the capital cost and the revenue is used to pay off the debt. From an operating perspective, all we need to do is to provide enough subsidies to tilt the environment in their favour, to be viable and successful. That might mean free land or better feed-in-tariff delivering better revenue from the energy sale for the renewable energy projects that you come up with.

FrICE programme does not require external support forever. It is only needed for a short period of time – till the project pays off its debt and generates free output, till you bootstrap yourself out of the loop into the free economy.

A good option will be to divert subsidies being currently provided to other sectors and feed them into these projects. Financially speaking, I do not see a massive government commitment here, for what we plan to achieve".

George continued, "However, let us keep in mind

that we are going to progressively move towards a free economy. The traditional source of income for the government is the tax on transactions. This will progressively reduce as more and more sectors become cost free. This might mean that the level of social services that we currently provide is likely to reduce.

I am concerned over dwindling tax revenues while still having to maintain services during the transition. It must be a controlled ascent up this cost-free heaven. One small misstep and you are in hell. All you need is a week without electricity or water or hospitals; the people are up in arms and your FrICE concept is out of the window".

"You are right", replied Palucci. "We need to look into this carefully. One positive aspect is that while the state revenue drops, the cost price index will also drop. For instance, once energy becomes free, it will be at zero cost. The basic wage or other social service support does not have to cater for energy and will be adjusted to reflect that. So progressively as sectors go cost free, the cost of living reduces and our need for support funds should progressively diminish.

We need to design it in such a way that the need for social security support is in sync with the commodity becoming cost free and the associated loss of tax revenue. We will be staring at a disaster if it goes the other way where we have no tax dollars to address the still existing social security needs".

"I think Treasury needs to maintain a buffer to offset any such scenario. We need to do some good quality modeling on the likely scenarios and find the sweet spot", said George.

Meg asked, "The next issue I had was about the business model and structure of the NFPs. During the presentation, I explained how we want public participation to drive the FrICE infrastructure development. We want the general public to be excited by the FrICE initiatives, to participate in the FrICE projects, to invest in the project and receive a good return on their investment".

George responded, "Yes. I do remember you saying that this public support will be crucial in making this project a political positive. I totally agree with you on the fact that it is only when people are behind these initiatives that we have a decent chance of success".

"Thank you", said Meg and continued, "To that end, in our model, the NFPs raise seed capital, say 30% of the project value, from the general public. The NFPs raise the remaining funds as commercial loans from financial institutions.

We design the programme such that the NFPs will pay a better than market rate as interest to the public investors. This will make sure that these projects are well received and are viewed favourably by the general public".

"Okay, so what is your issue with this structure?" asked George.

"Well, I just need some clarification. Will the public investors be treated as shareholders? If so, will they have the power to retain the not-for-profit in the revenue stream even after all the debts have been paid off. We do not want them to hang in there and perpetuate the profit model that was only put in place to become debt free".

George responded, "I wouldn't really worry about the structure. We could treat the NFP as a Company limited by guarantee. That model would be very suitable for a not-for-profit organization.

Or we could treat it as a social enterprise that applies commercial strategies to maximize improvements in financial and social domains".

Claire said, "We could just opt for a debenture issue to raise the capital from the public. That way, their contribution is treated more as a term loan with no ownership over the company.

Or we could explore the option of non-voting shares".

George said, "Or we could set up the investment contract such that the company will not pay any further returns after the stated time of ten years. That way, people have a bigger incentive to withdraw their money and invest it in the next FrICE venture. And the NFP is also under the pump to return the money and make the enterprise cost free and self-driving.

"Look, there are various options to ensure that the people get their returns and walk away with their investment with no further say in the enterprise. There are many options for us to make this debt-repayment model work. So, it will not be an issue".

Round Table – FrICE Board

Meg said, "The next item I want to table is the issue of taking this idea upstairs. Which is the best way to pitch this idea and sell it to the cabinet?"

Palucci responded, "This is going to be a big challenge for us. We will need a solid 'what is in it for me' for the politicians to take the bait".

Meg said, "When I opened the presentation, I talked about Atlantis. It is evident that adopting FrICE early makes a country a dominant global force, economically, politically and militaristically. If we are not one of the early adopters, we risk global subservience".

"That is great. But why would a politician still want to stick their neck out and propose such a major change with inherent risks? Wouldn't they be better off sticking to the routine, and harvest votes the traditional way?" asked Claire.

George said, "I wouldn't peg all politicians that

low. I believe most of them come into public life for a cause, to make it better for the people. Over a period of time, some may get corrupted or cynical and lose faith, but many still would recognize a real improvement opportunity and would support it".

Palucci said, "Getting back to the sales pitch, once this concept is published, the genie will be out of the bottle; the general populace will be aware of this concept and they will want FrICE".

"Care to spell it out?" said Claire.

Palucci responded, "Most people are not in love with what they are doing for a living, their job. They mostly do it to put food on the table, so to speak – to make money, to buy things that are essential to survive, as a minimum.

If you ask someone what their dream is, you might find that they would like to retire from their work and sit on a beach. Not sure if someone can sit on the beach forever, but that is the lure of walking away from their day job.

Now when FrICE tells them that they never have to work for a living and that all material things that they want can be had for free, that is pretty much a license to quit their job and sit on the beach all day. So, when they realize that this solution is available, believe me, there is going to be pressure on the representatives to fast track the same".

Claire responded, "You need to consider the scenario where people do not believe that FrICE is possible. The concept of 'nothing is for free' is deeply ingrained in the public psyche".

Ivan agreed. "True. The older generation will struggle with it much more than the younger generation. Especially when the FrICE concept is socialized among the younger generation, they will grow up with the idea that there is a clear plan to make every material thing free. The younger generation will be much more amenable to the concept and will be pushing for it".

Palucci said, "So, we agree that people will want it and what the people want is what the politicians will want, in an ideal world. On that basis, I believe that the politicians will push for FrICE.

On the other hand, we also know the risk of not implementing FrICE. The early adopters have a significant advantage; they are likely to dominate the global economic scenario. Those that do not adopt FrICE will become economic slaves and will live under the economic and military dominance of the early adopters. When FrICE concept is out there, when the general populace is aware of this concept, they will also be aware of this risk of not doing FrICE. And people will bring pressure on the politicians to act on the same. If not, they will hold the politicians responsible for that missed opportunity, the economic slavery, due to their inaction today".

"Sounds good. If you were to do an elevator pitch for FrICE, how would it go?" asked Ivan.

Meg responded, "I will keep it simple. I would say FrICE makes all material things free for everyone. Free energy, free food, free manufactured goods from shoes to TVs, umbrellas to furniture to cars and so on.

With FrICE, people do not need to work anymore. They can do whatever they wish and follow their passion. All of their material needs will be met, for free.

Countries that adopt FrICE early will have a significant advantage; they will dominate the global economic scenario. They will also be the dominant military force globally. And those that do not adopt FrICE will become economic slaves, living under the economic and military dominance of these early adopters.

We have the proverbial pot of gold at one end of the rainbow – free everything for everyone. On the other end, we have potential slavery. Which way do you want to go?

The choice is yours".

"Alright. Looks like we have a reasonably convincing sales pitch for the politicians. Let us come to the next part. You are talking about the need for a multi-partite, multi-faceted board to run FrICE. How do you justify the need for this board?" asked Ivan.

Meg responded, "Well, this is a long-term project that is likely to run over fifty years. Governments will change in that time frame. The party in power and the opposition will be in and out of government, possibly multiple times in that time frame. However, this project needs to go on. We need stability for this project to succeed. We need policies that will transcend politics of the day. We cannot have transient vagaries of the government of the day destabilizing this project.

Hence, we need a stable multi-partisan and somewhat independent FrICE Board, not dissimilar to the central banks in many countries, to direct and oversee FrICE initiatives".

"Okay, what are your thoughts on the structure of this board?" asked George.

"The board will be made up of representatives from the three arms of the government – the Legislative, Judiciary and the Executive. We will also have representation from the various political parties and experts from public policy, legal, education, economy, technology and other relevant domains. The board will be supported by expert technical committees from the various departments and the industry", responded Meg.

"Looks like a lot of seats on the board – sounds a tad heavy to me but carry on", said George.

"The board will be assigned a vision, mission, guidelines and a charter to successfully implement FrICE".

"Interesting. Any sample guidelines?"

"A key guideline will be to allow the market to drive FrICE as much as possible. The FrICE board will support FrICE initiatives primarily through policies, codes and legislation to direct outcomes as and where necessary.

The guidelines will direct the FrICE board to adopt a leverage funding approach, to utilize incentives and subsidies such as tax breaks, insurance, low-interest or interest-free loans, rent rebates and so on to promote FrICE initiatives. In rare circumstances, the board may use cash injections as part of leverage funding to facilitate preferred outcomes".

"That means the board is dependent on the government of the day to pass the necessary policies, codes and legislation or to gain the requisite subsidies", responded George.

"Yes and no. When we initiate FrICE, the strategy and general direction is well defined. The charter will identify the need for typical interventions such as policies, codes, legislation and subsidies that are likely to arise. Guidelines will also define the boundaries of such interventions.

The board will formulate the implementation details in consultation with experts in the relevant field. Any proposed intervention within the defined boundaries will be considered pre-approved and the legislature will pass it. Where extraordinary interventions are required, the board will have to approach the government of the day and get necessary approvals".

"Looks like we are proposing a structure that runs on its own with minimal oversight from the elected representatives of the day", said Ivan.

"We do not want the board to be losing focus on FrICE outcomes due to political exigencies of the day. However, we will have a mechanism through which the elected representatives take control of the board and change the charter. The government of the day can suspend, amend or rescind the FrICE initiative with a four-fifths majority in both the houses at any time", responded Meg.

"Isn't that too steep? I mean a four-fifths majority may be ... If we are asking for that kind of a majority, then shouldn't we have at least the same level of majority commitment when we kick off FrICE. Are we going to get it?" asked Claire.

"Why don't we keep it simple and propose a voting mechanism of say a two-thirds majority in both houses to establish the board and for any subsequent intervention?" suggested Ivan.

"I think it is a better idea to table this and leave it to the politicians. Let them decide on what is likely to give the best stability for FrICE. But I agree with you; whatever majority we want from the legislature to amend FrICE should be the majority we need to formulate FrICE", said George.

CHAPTER 19

The Cabinet

It was halfway through the cabinet presentation that Meg realized that the Secretariat was doing the heavy lifting. Most of the queries that came up were handled by the relevant departmental representative. Initially, Meg found this slightly irritating and was feeling cut off, but it slowly dawned on her that the Secretariat was sold on the idea; they were adopting it as their own and were stepping up to defend it. It was clear to her that this was a minor step towards the success of the FrICE concept.

Prior to the cabinet presentation, the core team of Meg, Palucci and a few secretaries had gotten together to decide on the strategy for the presentation. They had agreed that they would take a two-step approach. The primary presentation would paint the big picture, for that was what would really matter to the cabinet. If required, a secondary, more detailed presentation will be arranged to take the ministers through the specific details.

"I think we should kick off on the concept just as you did in our presentation", Claire said to Meg. "Talk about free everything for everyone. Mention specifics like free energy, free food, free cars, shoes, TVs, umbrellas. Keep it relatable to the common person, for they are the ones who matter to our politicians.

Once you have done that you might want to mention that it is limited to material things that have been around for a while, not new ideas or things.

By now, they would have grasped the potential benefits. Let us reinforce it by explaining how people will benefit, how they will love it and how this is the pot of gold at the end of the rainbow".

"I disagree", said George. "Once you explain the free everything for everyone concept, the primary question in everyone's mind would be 'how'. I mean, this has been deeply embedded in all of us. If you talk of the benefits now, they will still have an internal dialogue running that keeps asking 'but how is this possible'. So, I think we should go with that as the next piece".

"Okay. You take a simplistic approach for this segment saying machines make things. Automated machines make things without people. If we have free energy and free automated machines, all things can be made for free", said Claire.

"I think that will be a good and simple opening. Then you can go through the steps of making the automated machines free", George agreed.

"I will state that machines are made of metal and synthetics like plastic. I will explain the debt-repayment model for energy and show how we get to free energy in less than ten years. And I will explain how we get to free ore, free metal and free automated machines using the same method. I can close by stating that with free automated machines and free energy, we can make everything for free", said Meg.

"And then you come to the risk and reward aspects of FrICE", said George.

"I am not sure about this George", said Claire. "I think we should bring Atlantis right at the start, right after we say cost-free agriculture and manufacturing", and turning to Meg, "I liked your structured approach in our presentation. I think that would be the way to go. By the way, tone down the Atlantis risk scenario. People don't like being threatened. Let us keep it subtle and get it across in a more factual manner. The cabinet will get the point".

After some deliberation, the group agreed on the same.

"And we close with the need for the FrICE board", said Palucci.

Meg came back to the present as Claire was

providing some clarification on the job transition scenario. A few ministers had wanted clarification on how the impacted people would be taken care of. As Claire started explaining how the transition would be funded, George had stepped in to provide some clarity on the structure of the NFPs and the funding arrangement.

Earlier questions were raised on the energy transition and the proposed shift from the current strategy. Meg could see the gears turning inside the ministers' heads assessing the political impact of what was being tabled. Ivan explained to the cabinet how the government's current strategy of leaning to natural gas would dovetail well with FrICE and what changes the government would need to make in divesting gas production.

Meg was surprised at how well the cabinet members seemed to absorb the concepts and the meaningful questions that came up from them. 'Well, you don't get to the top of your game for nothing. No wonder this is a sharp crowd,' she thought to herself.

Presently a query came up from the floor.

"Free everything for everyone. Sounds great? But what if I want twenty Ferraris? What if everyone wants only Ferraris? And twenty each? Is there going to be any differentiation or are we all going to have the same?" asked the minister.

Palucci stepped in and said, "First point is that Ferrari may not be making cars anymore unless they become a part of FrICE and start making cars for free. You are more likely to have Ferrari-like cars, with similar specifications, made by NFPs, as long as there is a demand. So, if you want one, you may have one for free.

You can have as many Ferraris or fridges as you want. As you ask for more, the automated manufacturing complex will make it for you. Just that they will be block chain registered against your account, and at some point, you will need to recycle them, at end of their life".

"Won't we be overrun by demand from each and every person worldwide?"

"I seriously doubt it", said Palucci, "People do not accumulate or hoard things more than their real needs, especially when they are readily available for free".

George stepped in and said, "I will ask you something. In the last few minutes, how many breaths did you take?"

The minister's eyebrows went up. It looked like that the minister had gotten the point. George continued on for the less perceptive, "You could have taken a hundred, as air is free. You only took what you needed, mainly because air is free, and you did not look at it as a restricted and limited resource.

For human bodily needs, the demand is always limited to what the human body can consume. We will only take twelve to twenty breaths a minute. We will only consume a hamburger for a meal, not a hundred".

Palucci stepped in and said, "If we are talking of other material needs, humans tend to hoard or covet under a couple of situations. One is when there is a perceived shortage. When there is an abundant supply and no shortage, there will be no mad rush to accumulate or hoard. How many TVs, couches or washing machines will you take, if they are for free? Just what you need or a hundred? Under FrICE, you will only view the material for its utility value and procure accordingly.

The other situation is when the material has a perceived value, as in keeping up with the Joneses. But when FrICE is able to deliver the same appliance or gadget, for free, to you and your neighbour, that item will not have a perceived value based on its uniqueness. It will be just down to its utility value.

Where you want a material thing for its aesthetic value, like a painting or sculpture or a performance, that has inherent artistic, creative value, it will not be free and will fall outside of the FrICE spectrum", concluded Palucci.

"Alright. That makes sense", said the minister.

CHAPTER 20

FrICE Kick Off

As Meg was about to get back to the next slide which talked about the need for FrICE board, the Prime Minister, who had been quiet for most of the session, cleared her throat and said, "Okay, it is obvious that this is a big idea. How long does it take to make everything free for everyone?"

Palucci responded by saying, "Modelled estimates indicate it may take around fifty years".

"Great. I most probably will be dead by then. I will certainly not be around as the Prime Minister. And we will not be the ruling party for the next fifty years, for sure, even though that would be nice", she smiled looking at the cabinet colleagues.

"Look, it is evident that this is not a one party, one government initiative. First thing is we take a multi-partite approach and that means getting the other side in here, taking them through this and getting agreement on whether we want to do this, and if so, how do we go about getting this done".

"That is assuming that only these political parties are still going to be dominant in the next fifty years. Who knows what could come up in that period of time?" said the Treasurer.

"That's true", replied the Prime Minister, "But we can only work with what we have and know today. So, we will need to go with that".

Meg cleared her throat and said, "Ma'am, we have a slide on exactly what you have identified. It is true that this initiative will transcend parties and will spread over the aegis of multiple elected governments. Hence the proposal we have is as follows". Meg took the cabinet through the FrICE board concept. The cabinet seemed to be receptive of the FrICE board idea.

"We want the other side to be brought in. Which is the best way to proceed?" asked the Prime Minister.

Palucci said, "This topic has already seeped out into the political landscape. Members from both sides have already started asking questions wanting to know what is going on.

Here is my suggestion. Ministers have an off-the-record chat with their counterparts in the shadow cabinet. They will contact us to get some clarity. We will take them individually or in very small groups through the concept and the details. This way we can address and clarify any issues that people may have with FrICE".

"Sounds like a plan. I want you guys to form a team and get busy on this right away", the Prime Minister said and continued, "We will organize for a meeting, that is us the leadership group and our counterparts in the opposition, in a couple of weeks. We should get an idea of how things are likely to progress, politically, by then. Based on that, we can slot the multi-partite meeting and presentation in a months' time for the big crowd".

"Would it be better if we conduct a survey and get a feel for what people think of this idea", Palucci suggested.

"The concept is radical, to say the last. People are set in the theory that nothing is for free. I am not sure that we are going to get a realistic representative response from such a survey", responded George.

The Treasurer said, "Let us take a different tack. Let us seep this concept out to the public. Nothing to do with the government yet, but through an arm's length consultancy. We create the necessary chatter out there on this concept, in all channels: print, radio, TV and on social media. If asked, there is a 'no comment' from the government. Makes it all the more real while not committing us to anything.

We can then do the survey and may get a much more realistic response. And this exercise will also help to bring the opposition around".

"One last thing", said the PM. "I want this initiative to be clearly attributed to these young people", pointing to Meg, "in all marketing activities. That this idea originated from Belgrave High, and that Meg is part of our team actively engaged in this project, to make this idea happen".

CHAPTER 21

Emma

The lake was massive. It went on and on for hours. The women were lounging on the top and got slightly roasted by the sun. Presently they decided to get back in. It was still a couple of hours on the boat and another hour by road till they reached Siem Reap.

Emma had turned a deepish red and started applying some sunscreen on. "This is going to hurt tomorrow", she said. Meg turned around and said, "I told you so", with a comfortable smile, for you can play this "I told you so" comfortably with school friends, even if you meet them after twenty-five years.

"Miya is wrapping up in India and coming back to Melbourne", said Meg.

"Yeah, I saw her post. Why is she? Not happy in India?"

"Well, looks like she has achieved what she wanted to, there. Probably looking for a fresh start and why not back home?"

"Oh yes. A fresh start. Wouldn't we all love one",

Emma paused and said, "Not you, for sure. Wow, you are the miracle lady. Seriously, how did you manage that? Getting FrICE through? Believe me when I say this, it is not easy. I couldn't even scratch the surface".

"I agree, it is not easy, and no, I didn't do it. I was just a small lever who instigated it. I think it was just fortuitous; all the stars lined up and things happened. Seriously, back then, I thought I had brought all these key people together, that I had convinced them of the value of FrICE and that I had been instrumental in making FrICE happen.

With years of experience, I just smile today. The concept sold itself, thanks to Morty and Iyer who took us there. When you struggle to convince a five-year-old, you lose all illusions on your capacity to change things", Meg smiled.

"Oh yes. How is the lovely little angel? You are missing Sam?"

"Yes, certainly. But I had to take this break. I had been going non-stop for the last two years and I was staring at a complete breakdown. Now that I am here, I worry about how Joe is going to manage with Sam. Oh well, he'll be okay. Tell me all about your story in California".

Emma made a face, let out a long sigh and said, "Well, it is certainly not a fairy tale".

***

As Emma entered the convention, she realized it was big, and it was crowded. Her contact had suggested that she attend it. 'A bitchin' place to meet people who really care,' was how her contact had put it.

As Emma started walking through the stalls, she realized she could do with a good cup of coffee and she presently walked to the food court nearby. The girl next to her, with a head of shocking pink hair, smiled at her and asked, "What's your purpose in life?"

Emma picked up her jaw from the floor, recovered reasonably fast and said, "Free everything for everyone".

"Really, honey you need to wake up. The biggest issue facing us is climate change. We need to do everything we can to stop it and more importantly to reverse it", said the girl. Her t-shirt wanted to kill food miles.

Emma started to respond when the pink-haired girl continued on, "I want my food to be local. I do not want this crap from a thousand miles. Do you know the impact? Oh my God, do people not think about this? Every pack of food that travels a thousand miles is responsible for a big chunk of our global warming problem.

And the level of nutrient loss when the food is badgered and cajoled, picked early and gassed and whatnot before it is presented to you in your multi-national shopping centre. Do you have any idea what happens to your food?

It is killed. That is what happens to your food.

We need to go back to our roots", she said, "I want my bread to be made by my local baker using local ingredients. My avocados to be picked off the tree that morning and that is how I want my avo-on-toast. We should start living in our small communes where people know each other and care for each other. And we need to kill the big corporations and start feeding the local small business".

After multiple attempts, Emma managed to get a word in edgewise. Emma started to explain the Free Ice Cream concept in a concise manner. She came up to "free energy for all" in the third sentence when she was rudely interrupted by the food miles killer.

"Do you have any idea on what you are talking about? Oh honey, this is not a technical problem. This is a social issue. We need to shoot the pigs, the one-percenters, the MNC suits in their Manhattan corner offices. They are the problem. Inequality is the issue here".

Emma wanted to explain that with free clean energy, food miles were not an issue anymore. That long-distance transport will use clean energy with no associated carbon dioxide emissions.

Emma wanted to explain that with free economy, all food was going to be free. That the local produce from the farmers market would cost the same as a long-distance, processed food in the supermarket shelf. That the MNCs may no longer be players in that space. That it would provide a level playing field and people could buy local or remote produce based on their preference.

Emma noticed that the pink-haired girl had a "food miles" message on the back of her t-shirt as well.

Picking up her coffee and walking towards a row of stalls, Emma bumped into a tall angular bespectacled man and before she realized she was deep in conversation with him. To be fair, it was more of a monologue.

"Do you agree that each and every action of ours has an impact. Something somewhere changes to some extent due to our action".

Emma could not really argue with that.

"We need to really consider that before we jump into a so-called solution. There are some here that are planning to flood the Mojave with solar panels. Are they aware of the ecological disaster they are promoting? Absolutely not. And when I go and try to get some sense into them, they look at me like I am some sort of a crazy person".

Emma did not want to comment on that.

"Don't they understand that cutting off sunlight to the land is no different to contaminating the soil with other pollutants. They basically kill the soil. Nothing can grow there. The soil cannot sustain life".

Emma kept quiet, but her face must have betrayed the question pounding inside her head: "but isn't that a desert and nothing grows there anyway".

"Think of the rattler and its food chain from the rodents to the insects and so on. All of this is going to be impacted. Big solar farm and other structures can alter the flow of water across the land and can possibly impact on the types and location of the native flora and fauna".

Emma continued to not really argue with that.

"And a hundred years from today, people will realize what a major disaster this has been and will have to undo all of it. Better to stop it now".

At last, Emma broke down and said, "So, you are saying that we should not do anything because of a remote possibility that it may have an impact later?"

"Absolutely not", came the reply. "Any proposal has to have a detailed assessment of its ecological and environmental impact. In there, they should identify all the possible impact issues and provide a detailed management plan".

It sounded very reasonable to Emma.

And the man continued, "and we will decide on

what will be approved. The current nonsense has to stop. The department is a toothless tiger. It is time for NFPs like us to step in and enforce real accountability".

As the man moved away, the back of his t-shirt said Ecountability in bold red.

"That is a perfect demonstration of what a power monster is". Emma turned to see the person smile at her and say, "New to the convention, are you? Your first time?" Emma nodded.

"Well, there are two kinds of people here", the lady said. "The romantic fools with stars in their eyes and 'save the earth' solutions in their bags. And then of course there is the power group trying to 'rule the earth' either through regulation or money. Believe me, both are the same and they loathe each other".

"Heather", the lady proffered her hand, "and let me guess, you belong to the first group".

Emma shook Heather's hand and agreed.

"I'm a consultant for the energy industry", Heather said. "I keep coming to this circus every year and I have to say it keeps getting more exciting every year. So, tell me about your 'save the world' story". Emma gave Heather a very short version from free energy to free everything.

Heather looked like a seasoned pro who had seen it all. Heather said, "Honey, I am a seasoned Pro. I have seen it all".

Heather took Emma around the convention. There were stalls and displays pertaining to a range of "green" issues ranging from ecological commerce to finance to accountability, environmental tariff to trading, carbon footprint to finance to offset to neutrality to food miles and so on. Further, there were stalls on the anarchy stream of various groups attempting to eliminate either the ruling class or the multi-nationals or inequality in the society through means ranging from peaceful protests to the other extreme.

The second amendment stalls were at the far end.

CHAPTER 22

Solar in California

Back in Los Angeles, Heather had asked Emma to come to the high school auditorium for a meeting. Driving up to the school, Emma could see the city hall spire in a distance. Arriving at the high school carpark, Emma noticed Heather talking to a few people and presently joined them.

After brief introductions, the group moved in to one of the meeting rooms in the auditorium. Heather stood up, welcomed everybody to the meeting and said, "Let me clarify why we are here. As a group, all of you seem to have a common interest. All of you have an active interest in installing clean energy generators in California.

Your group seems to be interested in solar as the solution. Understand that within solar you seem to have differences in the technology options. Some seem to prefer the PV solution while others prefer the solar thermal solution.

Do not be offended when I say this, but the most important common attribute that I can see in this group is that you all seem to be clueless on how to implement your ideas. I have briefly spoken to most of you individually. What I have gathered is that you have this great idea to save this world from the polluters and other greedy monsters and you have no idea as to what you are up against; no idea as to how city hall works; no idea as to who your competition is, and of course no idea as to how to beat your competition. You are what I would call cannon fodder.

Understand that I am passionate about your solutions as much as you are. I was one of you ten years back, but", and Heather paused here for emphasis, "I have also learned over the last ten years. Today, I am older and wiser. I know the lay of this land. I have been engaging with city hall and other government bodies as a consultant for almost a decade. I know what is required of you. I know what needs to be done by you guys to have a reasonable chance of success.

Looking at you guys, I think I am your only hope. You have great ideas, the state wants the great ideas implemented, and the shortest distance between two points is not a straight line but a middleman, or a middle woman in this case".

A person at the far end of the table said, "Are you

suggesting that we engage you as our consultant?"

Heather said, "Yes".

"Would you support and guide us on a pro bono basis, no fees?" asked the person.

"No, there will be a consulting fee for my work", said Heather.

"Look Heather, we have come here with the solution not to make money out of it. We want to fix the global issues and our solution will do it. We have no commercial interest in the process. I cannot speak for others here, but I am not sure if I will be willing or able to pay you for what I believe is essentially work for a good cause".

Heather replied, "Normally I would not touch what I classify as newbies", Heather pointed to everyone at the table, "people like yourself who come to the city to try and get your idea implemented. My preference is to let them try their luck, hit their heads against the brick wall for a couple of years. After that experience, half the crowd gives up and goes back to where they came from. The remaining few by then are absolutely ready for a consultant to step in and walk them through the maze.

Something happened this time. Not sure what it is. I must be getting soft. I looked at you people and something inside me snapped. You guys came here to do good. I did not want to see you going back feeling angry, puzzled and having lost faith in the goodness of this world. I did not want you to go through that carnage. I did not want to see the destroyed hopes and ambitions.

And that is the reason we are here today. I am not even charging you for my time at this meeting. Speaking of money, I am aware that most you may not have funds to engage me on a consulting basis. But that is not a problem. We build the consulting cost into the project and that way the project pays me, not you guys".

There was silence around the table.

"Okay, let us kick off. The state of California is kicking off its multibillion-dollar green earth programme. Most of you have probably visited this year's convention. All the players you found there are also going to be active participants in this programme.

You need to be able to sell your idea to the state and convince them to plonk all that money on your projects. In reality, that will not happen. If history is a good indicator, the state will hedge its bets and will distribute the funds far and wide. They call it better risk management. I call it the win for the lobbyist.

In the name of ecology and environment, there will be projects proposed and approved to try different technologies and methods for processing human waste. There will be interest groups pushing for localized sewage treatment with people claiming that what came from the local soil should go back to the local soil with minimal processing. There will be others who promote converting it to fertilizer and using it in agriculture and others for a deep ocean outfall.

And that is just the shitty end of things. There are going to be project proposals to store water, conserve water, minimize evaporation, effective irrigation, salinity, water table issues and of course to make fresh water.

As you can understand, the multibillion-dollar budget is nothing compared to the deluge of proposals on the table. Now, your proposal needs to stand out among this crowd. You need the ability to lobby the decision makers.

The upfront decision-making process is absolutely convoluted with complicated rubrics and matrices. Believe me when I say you will need a couple of PhDs to understand and comply with the requirements. However, a good understanding of who is who in the decision-making zoo is also critical.

You need to understand individual personal preference and who is able to swing whom one way or the other. You need to understand the various factions and blocks within the same party and who is actually pulling the strings and from where. Some of these key stakeholders may not even be on the decision-making committees.

You do not stand a chance here by yourself. The consultants and lobbyists are crucial".

Heather paused and said, "So, if anyone wants to go ahead and fight this windmill on your own, now is the time to leave. For the rest, we will continue with our strategy session".

The table kept quiet and stayed back.

CHAPTER 23

The Californian Knife

Meg and Emma moved out to the aft deck of the boat. There was still a couple of hours to Phnom Krom. The aft of the boat was under shade and cool with a brisk wind. Emma secured her hat and parked herself on the bench. Meg stood next to her stretching. Emma continued on with her experience in California.

Over the next few months, Emma and others agreed to join the lobby group. Emma stayed close to Heather and was able to see the carnage and the feeding frenzy that the tender unleashed. It was a frightening introduction to the power hungry, dog-eat-dog world of the commercial side of green solutions.

Emma could not see a conceivable pathway for her to introduce FrICE. She realized that her solution concept will not flow through this mayhem and that she will have to compromise. Their lobby group put together a proposal under the tutelage of Heather and submitted the same. In a few weeks' time, the tenders were opened and awarded. Emma's group submission got approved in parts.

The group managed to get some solar farms approved for construction. They were based on a commercial model with no option to go free. Their debt-repayment and free energy generation proposal was rejected.

The rest of the group seemed satisfied. 'Well, we got something after all our effort,' seemed to be the general consensus. Emma held back her disappointment and got to work. Managing the construction phase of the project was a learning experience for her. The solar farm came together with the usual hiccups and delays expected of any other construction project.

The group popped Champagne the morning they commissioned the farm and started pumping clean, green, renewable energy into the grid. The first few weeks of operation went reasonably well. And then the problem started. The solar farm started shutting down due to grid over voltage.

When queried, the technician explained it. "Electrical voltage is like water pressure. Electricity will only flow from a higher voltage to a lower voltage. When you generate electricity in your solar farm, that electricity has to be at a higher voltage than the grid. If the grid is at a higher voltage, you will not be able to pump electricity into the grid".

And when you are not pumping electricity into the grid, you are not making money. This started happening more and more often to the point where the farm was productive less than 50% of the time. Complaints to the network distributor were of no use. They in turn were blaming the increase to an increasing number of renewables feeding into their grid and were stating that there was nothing they could do.

With reduced productivity came reduced revenue and the solar farm struggled to meet payments. The operation was going in to the red and there was pressure mounting all around to do something. Heather came in as a saviour and organized for the farm to be offloaded.

"But wouldn't they have the same problem. Can we sell without full disclosure?" asked Emma.

"Darling, our job is to minimize damage to ourselves. We will make sure we do not do anything illegal. Relax, I know of people who can handle this for us".

The rest of the group agreed with Heather and the farm was offloaded to another company. Most of the group heaved a sigh of relief as they got out without being severely burnt, just mildly singed. While most of the group disbanded, Emma stayed in touch with her contacts in the power industry.

In the next six months, some disturbing information started coming Emma's way. Her solar farm had changed hands a couple of times and that there were some irregularities in the transactions. Interestingly, the issue of grid over voltage had been resolved once the farm was out of their hands; Emma was not clear how that happened. The mob that bought it from them had made a decent profit in that transaction. There was chatter that Heather had made a killing with that transaction and that someone high up in the network distributor was in the deal as well.

On reaching Siem Reap, Emma and Meg checked in to their accommodation, freshened up and came down to the lobby. The weather was beautiful. Both parked themselves in the lounge chairs among the tropical trees and shrubs out in the garden and ordered their Angkor beer.

Sipping her beer, Emma continued. She had confronted Heather seeking clarification on all the things she was hearing. Interestingly, Heather did not deny any of it. Instead, she just said, "Honey, you came here for some experience; to do some good, as you would put it. I think you have achieved both. Because of your effort, we now have another solar farm generating clean, green, renewable energy. It was your effort, your initiative, that made it possible.

Are you going to say no?"

Emma wasn't but asked Heather point blank if she had a role in the shady deal and if she had made money on the same.

"Honey, you are new in this theatre. But you are also richer today with the experience. You have dipped your toe into this pool of green solutions. You should share this lived experience with others in your life. You need to understand that I too share some of this pride in creating something green, for both of us will agree that without me your group would have gone nowhere.

You certainly did not come into this to make money. Who owns the farm and who makes money out of it is not really your concern, your main focus was to go green, agree?"

Emma did not respond.

Heather continued, "But I am an old hand in this space. Been around for a while. Need to make some money as well. So, I make a few dollars, so what. Why should that bother you, really?"

Heather did not even look at what she had done as being wrong. Emma was shaken by Heather's complete lack of remorse. She still wanted confirmation on the network distributor's role in the scam. "Who was it at the distributor? It has to be some people high up in their company, for sure", asked Emma.

Heather couldn't care less. "Listen honey. Don't chase this. You will get hurt, big time. But I am okay to tell you some of the details because, believe me, you are not going to be able to do anything. This is a well-oiled machine and has been running smooth for a while. There is a demi-czar at the network distributor who manages the deal. He gets a big cut, people like me get small cuts, and most importantly, his company picks up assets at half the price. So, he is the golden boy over there".

Emma turned to Meg, placed her beer on the rattan and said, "I started digging around and you won't believe what I found. That demi-czar at the network distributor was none other than our Karan".

Meg's jaw dropped.

CHAPTER 24

Miya, the Indian Solution

Miya was paying off the tuk-tuk as Chen was grabbing the bags. Meg and Emma went out to give them a hand. After initial hugs, Miya and Chen checked in, freshened up and came down to the lobby and plonked themselves with their beer in the garden chairs for a long chat with Meg and Emma.

Emma asked Miya of her experience in India.

"How was it? Tough? Challenging?"

"Oh my God, it was sheer madness at first, but I think I have fallen for that place now", Miya said with a smile.

Working in India was an eye opener for Miya. She had taken up a job with an international consultancy. The consultancy firm threw her in at the deepest end possible. As a raw graduate, out of university, Miya expected better mentorship and guidance, but it was not to be.

"Here is your access card", said her team leader,

"You get in through Gate 8, go through security and the client will be there to meet you".

There was not just one security screening. By the time Miya reached Gate 8, she had gone through two security screenings where her access card and other papers were scrutinized and the third one was a thorough pat down.

And the client was not there to meet her. Having waited for around twenty minutes, Miya called up her team leader to inform that the client hadn't showed up for the meeting. She was asked to hang around, check with the office attendants and figure out when the client may show up and wing it from there.

And thus, Miya got introduced to India. The inscrutable head shake that could mean a yes or a no or an okay, the concept of flexi-time, the heat, the crowds, the queue that flared at the head, the zig zag line that was the closest distance between any two points, the list was endless.

Her bosses in the consultancy firm seemed to be adopting a Western approach to problem solving in India and that was not getting her anywhere. She could not get straight answers from any part of the government bureaucracy and she was running from pillar to post to nowhere. Slowly, over time, Miya figured out the lay of the land; on how to get things done in India. She started developing business contacts and relationships. Miya was in the renewable energy sector of her consultancy business and was well placed to start pushing aspects of the FrICE concept.

Miya replied to Emma, "Of course, it was challenging. With every step moving up, you would slide down a couple. Once you say we need to deliver free power, there will be a faction that will say free power is already a reality among the rural population. Then they will want to know how that is going to translate to more votes. It was painful trying to explain the FrICE concept of free energy, which is absolutely cost free, against their concept of free energy, which is a government subsidy. And the factions wouldn't care; all they cared was about the votes".

"Well, at least they are true to their profession. What else is a politician expected to chase?" said Meg.

"You would think. How about money. Oh my God", said Miya. "The moment we start talking free energy, there is a factional war on who should get it. I could be standing in a corner screaming that it needs to be free for everyone and it would have had absolutely no effect. Their motto was free energy to selected industries – selected by them and you could almost smell the kickbacks".

"Throughout this madness, the Prime Minister's Office was a refuge. I would go and cry to them and they would do the 'there, there' till I settled down and throw me right back in the zoo", said Miya with a wry smile.

"So, how far did it veer off course? Is there any semblance to FrICE? Are they going to be able to deliver free everything to everyone?" asked Emma.

"I am not sure. Certain aspects of FrICE have been implemented though not necessarily as we would have expected. It has delivered a lot of value to the local population. It has also made 'select' industries, companies and families richer. Let us say it is a mixed bag".

"Solar has taken off in a very big way. The government has promoted rooftop solar with a decent relief structure – 50% as tradeable carbon offset certificates, and for lower income classes, they gave 20% as rebate and 25% as interest-free loan repayable over five years, only 5% investment out of hand. There was a huge uptake as the feed-in-tariff was pretty decent as well, giving people an opportunity to go green and make some money.

Of course, the relief structure applied only for approved brands and retailers. A 'selected' few manufacturers get on the approved list and that was a minor scam by itself".

"Did it upset you that what could be a pure altruistic scheme gets tainted like this?" asked Emma.

"Sure did, initially, till I was given some 'advice' by one of my political mentors", said Miya.

Meeting Chauhan in the lift, by chance, changed everything for Miya. Miya and her friend were talking of her school Free Ice Cream Project. Chauhan had overheard the conversation and interestingly he had heard of Free Ice Cream Project as well, a few years back. As they were leaving the lift, Chauhan confirmed that Miya was talking about the same project that he had heard of and had ordered Miya to show up at his office the next day.

Miya figured out that Chauhan was a top political appointee at the Prime Minister's Office. After months of repeatedly hitting her head against brick walls of varied shapes and sizes, she couldn't have asked for a better break, or so she thought.

After many a session with Chauhan discussing the Free Ice Cream concept in detail, the discussion veered to how best to present it to the top.

"Let me play the devil's advocate", said Chauhan. "The people making these decisions are some of the most powerful people in this country. Most of the decision will be in the hands of the cabinet that is predominantly made up of politicians. The senior administrative staff will certainly have a say and so will the dominant industrialists, especially when your plan involves making things free".

Chauhan stayed quiet for a while and said, "Dominant religious and caste-based groups may also have a say, but I don't think this project will *be* impacted by that", Chauhan paused for a moment and said, "Well, I don't think they will have an impact, but you never know and that is the beauty of it. Most of the dominant religious and caste-based groups are active in politics anyway. So, we can club them as politicians.

Now don't get me wrong. I have nothing against politicians. I am one myself. Some are visionaries. Most of them have a clear place and need in a democracy. They are supposed to represent people, and in their own convoluted way, they do. They chase votes and one way to get the votes is by listening to people and giving them what they want.

So, if we must make this concept a success, we should get the politicians interested in this and get them to see that this will get them votes. So, let us ask ourselves those questions and try to package this in a positive manner.

The first question is who are my voters?" asked Chauhan.

"Well, over 70% of the population resides in rural areas and is predominantly engaged in agriculture", said Miya.

"Bingo. So, how will this help them?"

"Well, most farmers need electricity to pump water to the fields. If the electricity is free, will it not be a good idea?" asked Miya.

"The reality is that most farmers are getting electricity for free now. Most of the state governments do not charge farmers for electricity. States that do, do not enforce collection. By default, over the years, things have slid down that way. So, that is not going to be a win for you".

"Are all farmers in all villages getting free electricity all the time?"

"Well, certainly not. It is due to the fact that we are deficient in generation capacity and the fact that you can only dole out so much free stuff before your treasury goes dry", said Chauhan.

"That is an opportunity for us. We can provide free electricity to all farmers, in all villages, all the time through FrICE. No more power cuts. Will that sell?" queried Miya.

"It will certainly help".

"Okay how about free energy for the farm tools like tractors and things?"

"Hmm … it is an option to put on the table".

"If we were to pitch it in such a way that we produce all this free energy and are able to generate clean fuel, say hydrogen, to power all farm tools and give it to all farmers for free?"

"Getting warmer".

"And we could also use the hydrogen to manufacture urea and fertilizer and give it free to the farmers", said Miya.

"So, now we are giving free electricity all the time, to all farmers and villages. We are also giving them free hydrogen-based portable power, to run the farm machinery and light up their villages. And, with free hydrogen, we are going to produce and give the farmers free fertilizer. I think the pitch just got a lot warmer", said Chauhan. "I think we are missing one crucial element to wrap up this agricultural package. How about including free tractors and farm equipment as well?"

"Done. Let us include that as well. By the way, this initiative can also move India away from being an energy-dependent country. With all the electrical power we generate, we can produce hydrogen and reduce our oil dependence. Our transport infrastructure can be converted to hydrogen-powered engines and that can be done over say twenty years if we all push together. Further, we could also sell hydrogen to overseas markets. There is a need for clean energy out there", responded Miya.

"Agreed. That would be a big selling point", said Chauhan and continued, "One important aspect we are not touching upon is how political parties can monetize this programme".

"Really? Why would you want to corrupt the process? Why not keep it clean?" asked Miya.

"Young lady, you seem to be missing the point. How do you think political parties fight elections? With money. And where does the money come from? From people, as donations, and from businesses, as 'contributions', and these contributions are a big part of the election funds".

"Are you saying all of these 'contributions' get spent on elections?"

"Absolutely not. As money passes through hands, some of it will stick. So, a lot of people and families in the contribution chain get very wealthy as well".

"Is there any way we can do the project straight, without corrupting it?"

Chauhan said, "Let me assure you of this. FrICE, by itself, is a huge concept. Getting that through will be a herculean task. If you try to go for a 'FrICE with clean hands' project, there is no way this will fly. So, let us take it one battle at a time. Remember Hitler and the Russian front?

Let us pitch it as *Free Everything to Everyone*. We paint a picture of the agricultural package that we discussed. We include free energy, water, fertilizer, tractors and farm equipment as well. We will show how it will benefit farmers, how it will translate to votes and how it will also fill up our election coffers. We don't have to mention palms being greased; they will catch up on that easy".

Observing Miya's pained look, Chauhan said, "Let us look at it this way. Through this project, you are getting something, a kick-start on your free economy project. They are getting a few things: some development work to boast of, some funding for elections and some funds for themselves. This way everyone is happy. And in the long run, when you manage to make everything for free, it will be interesting to see if that stops people craving for money".

When submitted to the cabinet, the concept of an independent FrICE board did not fly. Selected aspects of the concept were adopted. The Prime Minister's Office redesigned the solution package. Huge parcels of work were generated.

When FrICE was officially communicated, everyone jumped in: commercial operators, NFPs and the government departments as well, in some instances. There was frenzied activity in the New Delhi political and business circle. Factional heavy weights and consultants across the political spectrum jumped into the fray with various multi-national companies for a piece of the action.

Vested interests made sure that the barriers to

entry for NFPs was fairly high. In spite of that, some NFPs made it through with the debt-repayment model. Many of the government subsidies favoured select commercial sector operators who did not necessarily adopt the free energy strategy. BSE Index went through the roof. Some people made a lot of money.

Miya's profile within her consulting firm shot up. She was under further pressure from her firm to push and promote their existing clients into these projects.

"So, what is the overall picture over there?" asked Emma.

"Now there is lots of energy available. There is a significant boost in the clean renewable power generation capacity. Rooftop solar is a big contributor for energy".

"So, is it predominantly solar over there?" asked Emma.

"Oh no. They have gone with clean, renewable combination of solar and wind. They have also gone big on nuclear. The 'Finestra' foundation had been talking to them for quite a while on this and they have gone ahead with a few of the new generation fission reactors that are considered to be very safe. Interestingly, they have pretty much eliminated human interaction in the operation of these reactors – not from a cost perspective but to eliminate the human error factor and make it safer.

One good thing that came out of this for FrICE Energy was that unused railway land was provided for free to the NFPs. So, one cost aspect was taken out of the equation. And that was probably my only true contribution in this process", Miya bowed.

"Why railway land?" asked Emma.

"The Indian Railways is one of the largest organizations in the country. As a matter of fact, it is one of the largest employers in the world. It is also the biggest landowner in the country. The land in their possession is bigger than many states of India. And a lot of it is unused, vacant land.

Land acquisition is one of the most expensive and time-consuming processes over there. If you start a project that requires land, it could be decades before the litigation is resolved by the judiciary and you are able to start the project.

I had this stroke of genius and put it across to the Prime Minister's Office, suggested they use the unused railway land for solar farms. They took it on board and actually implemented it. Using available railway-owned land is seen as a successful outcome as land acquisition time and cost have been eliminated. Gradually Indian Railways is transitioning to clean energy.

There is a big promotion of micro networks that are village based. This delivers power to villages while not adding significant 'wires and poles' distribution costs. A lot of the solar infrastructure is networked locally such that villages are covered a hundred percent. We also have a lot of micro hydrogen plants that are powered by the surplus electricity. The hydrogen is injected into the existing biogas systems that generate methane from animal waste.

India has not applied the FrICE concept to mining, due to political exigencies, but has applied it to metal recycling sector. With the available surplus energy, it has established carbon-free metal recycling factories and the factories are predominantly automated.

This focus on the recycling sector has had a huge impact. Indian imports of metal waste for recycling has taken off. Some 'selected' metal recyclers have been given permits to put up plants with free FrICE energy on offer. There is also an active NFP stream in this space producing free metal for downstream activities with block chain oversight.

Interestingly, this has had a domino effect. The abundance of metal availability and free energy has promoted the machine manufacturing sector in a big way. As per plan, the agricultural and farm equipment manufacturing sector has done very well. Most of the output, from the NFP stream, is delivered for free to the end user, the farmer. The commercial stream focuses more on exports.

Moreover, the small machine manufacturing sector that manufactures pumps, motors, gearboxes and industrial hardware such as actuators and drives has also had a big boost due to the FrICE initiative, to the point where India is the global leader in this sector.

This, in turn, has boosted up the light manufacturing sector as the machines and energy could be had for free, if they were FrICE registered, or at a lower rate for a commercial operation. Over and above the NFPs, select commercial operators in the F&B and FMCG (fast-moving consumer goods) manufacturing sectors, depending on incumbency, regional vote bank, indigenous and traditional agri businesses, and political family holdings, have also significantly benefitted from the initiative.

India has further promoted innovation in software solutions in a big way and has become a dominant global force in paid software and AI solutions for industrial automation. With an increased availability of these machines at a low or no cost, and robust technology capability in IT and AI, Indian Light Manufacturing sector is currently booming, with more carbon–free, clean energy–powered, fully automated factories coming up in a big scale".

"And that is the state of play in India", Miya concluded.

CHAPTER 25

Meg, the Oz Solution

Nader flew in from the United States and joined them the next morning at Siem Reap.

The group spent a leisurely morning walking through Ta Prohm. The trees growing out of the ruins and the jungle surroundings were just breath-taking. Back at a café for lunch, the group wanted to know how things turned out in Australia.

"Well, I have been giving you guys a running commentary as we were going through the process", said Meg.

"Only till the cabinet presentation. What happened after that?" asked Chen.

"You are a good one to ask me. How come we didn't hear a peep from you all this while?" asked Meg.

"There are reasons. I will tell you later. Now you go first", responded Chen.

"Okay. I will give you an overview", said Meg.

***

The few weeks after the cabinet presentation were a flurry of activity.

Meg and Palucci made initial contact with select members of the Secretariat, Shadow Ministry and influential members and factional leaders in the lower and upper house and had scheduled meetings ranging from brunch at coffee shops to lunch sessions at restaurants.

Meg, Palucci, George and Ivan and a few others from the Secretariat were actively engaged in doing one-on-one sessions with select members. The idea was being presented as a hypothetical, but it was clear to the members that the idea was being seriously considered as the news of the cabinet presentation had been leaked.

These open meetings and visual presence further fanned the rumour flames around the capital. The media became more aware that something big was coming up. The government spokesperson kept leaking information in small bites keeping the media interest alive.

The opposition leadership team was briefed on the content. Informal meetings between ministers and their opposition counterparts were initiated. These meetings were facilitated by the departmental secretaries. The outcome was positive; leadership teams from both parties were in favour of going ahead with FrICE, provided the wider cabinet, both houses of the parliament and the people were also in favour of FrICE.

The cabinet and opposition agreed that the people need to be presented the news highlighting the positives. An external consultant was engaged to design and deliver the marketing strategy. The key message to the public was that they were going to get everything for free in the near future. And they can also invest in the initiative and make some money today. The marketing campaign was initiated. Initial results indicated a positive uptake from people.

In a few weeks' time, Meg and the team organized a presentation session for all the select members they had touched base with earlier. They ran a detailed presentation on FrICE including all the queries and responses. Priming everyone over the previous few weeks was effective; all seemed to be for FrICE.

The marketing campaign reached peak coverage and penetration. The government and the opposition had their ears to the ground. Constant polling indicated positive uptake on the people front.

The wheels were set in in motion and the drums started rolling. The media joined the hype. It was all systems go. The government went public and Australia officially kicked off the Free Ice Cream Economy project.

Meg said, "I should say that the marketing campaign was brilliant. We had a surge of approval from the people and everything was positive from there on.

We have stuck to the debt-repayment model with investment from the public. The response has been good. We have constructed a combination of solar PV and wind farms to about 40% of the planned capacity. The people have ownership of these and benefit from these for the first ten years. The debt-repayment model also takes care of the impacted people, from traditional power. They benefit from these plants through the transition fund.

Australia has started moving towards a hydrogen economy. Salt caverns have been mined for gas storage. The government has installed the corresponding capacity of hydrogen generators, fuel cells and combined cycle hydrogen turbine power plants to address the intermittency of solar and wind.

Some international sale of hydrogen, as syngas and ammonia, has started. This is expected to be a big win for Australia as the rest of the world has started clamouring for clean energy. The fuel is also provided for free for those recipients that are part of FrICE, and block chain technology is adopted to demonstrate traceability and compliance.

Mining negotiations are near completion. The FrICE

board has selected the preferred tenderers to build, own and operate the mining complex. The successful tenderers have raised the seed funding from the public and the loans from financial institutions based on the debt-repayment model. They have purchased iron ore mines and copper mines and the required fully automated mining equipment to operate them. The mining equipment is almost automated. Drills, haul trucks and shovels are driverless. Blasting still requires some human input, albeit remote.

They are in the process of constructing the fully automated ore processing facility. With free electricity and portable hydrogen-based clean energy, the mine seems to be all set to start production in a few months.

The FrICE board has requested for an expression of interest from NFPs to build, own and operate a steel mill and a copper smelter in the region earmarked for the industrial complex. The response has been positive. Three different consortiums with people of significant experience in the respective fields have entered the fray as NFPs. All have either a collaboration or licensing arrangement with relevant process owners and/or global manufacturers in the respective domains".

"That is interesting. Why would commercial enterprises want to engage with and contribute to

FrICE? Aren't they killing the commercial model?" asked Emma.

"Who knows, it's possible that they are under the pump from their shareholders and investors to deliver on their corporate social responsibility. Maybe they can see the writing on the wall and want to be the first to transition", responded Meg and continued, "The FrICE board has also invited Expressions of Interest from NFPs to build, own and operate a heavy machinery manufacturing facility in the industrial complex. The facility will be geared to manufacture free machinery for the mining and metals manufacturing industries. We expect to have all of the heavy machinery rolling out for free in a few years from now".

"Impressive. Looks like you are on plan", said Chen.

"And I hear that you are way ahead", Meg responded to Chen with a smile.

CHAPTER 26

Chen, Asia Update

"I am not even sure what you do. All I can gather is that you are on the move all over Asia", said Emma.

Chen smiled and said, "I am in the same space as you guys. I tried to kick off FrICE in some of countries in Asia with varying levels of success.

In central Asia, we have a very interesting development. Interest groups have taken the FrICE concept and have kicked it off with minimal government involvement in countries with minimal natural gas reserves. Massive solar farms have come up under the debt-repayment model. And some countries are using their hydroelectric-friendly terrain to build pumped hydro capacity as energy storage for other countries generating renewable energy. This is FrICE implementation by NFPs on their own; no government involvement here. It is a space to watch, for sure.

South Korea has taken the FrICE lead in ship

building. They have set up a FrICE shipyard that will be delivering its first almost FrICE vessel within the next eighteen months. The ship is being built with free FrICE steel and free energy being brought in. The propulsion machinery is still from the market. So, there will be some cost associated with that. And the contract specifies free clean renewable fuel to run the ships for the next twenty years. So, it will be a huge reduction in cost of shipping. News is that the FrICE yard has orders for hundreds of vessels. Commercial shipping will not last long at this rate.

But the big news is obviously China. There should be no surprises here. They had been dominating the manufacturing sector even before FrICE, just by labour cost differential. They understood FrICE very well and acted on it".

"Of course, with their political structure, they can do whatever they want. No wonder they are ahead", said Emma.

"I don't think so", said Chen. "There are a lot of countries with similar political structures out there. Almost none has done what China has achieved".

"So, where are they?" asked Emma.

"To put it in simple terms, China is miles ahead. China did not adopt the FrICE board concept. That was to be expected. A select subcommittee, reporting directly to the central committee, has been set up to expedite FrICE.

For energy, China has adopted a combination of solar, wind, and nuclear power, similar to India. The difference is that all fossil fuel generators have been retired. China is almost at 100% clean generating capacity.

Today the power plants are free. Solar farms can be set up with no labour and material cost. China has standard template farms that can be installed and commissioned by robots – no humans required. As an exercise, they recently erected and commissioned a wind farm with only two people in the control tower, intervening and directing the robots.

Free mining machines have started rolling out, and free blast furnaces and smelters are ready as well. China is in the process of automating all mines, mills and factories. The expectation is that everything will be free for internal consumption, with enough surplus for the international market.

Very soon, you will see China decimate the global manufacturing market. You remember how the United States could not even manufacture masks during the last pandemic. All countries are going to be pushed in the same corner very shortly.

I think I will let you in on a secret. In emerging China, dominance is the catch word of the day, not benevolence", Chen concluded.

That evening, Meg, Miya, Emma and Chen celebrated turning forty-two that year. Nader had ordered a cake with forty-two candles on it. All four blew out the candles.

CHAPTER 27

The American Saga

The next day, the group took a trip to the nearby Phnom Kulen waterfalls. They had opted to hike the last couple of kilometres. While walking up, the discussion came around to developments in the United States.

Nader gave them an overview on the American status. The US had not adopted FrICE. There was a big push from the vested interests feeding the public with how the concept of FrICE was anti-American. They emphasized on and sold the value of the "American spirit" and "American individuality". The shock jocks were screaming on how FrICE would kill the greatest American invention, the "free market". Adam Smith rolled in his grave.

In the meanwhile, the US had not been able to bring back manufacturing. Businesses that outsourced their manufacturing to other countries, where labour was cheaper, stayed put; none came back. Lost jobs remained so. There were no new jobs in traditional manufacturing.

And US was dependent on other international players for all manufactured goods. With no major exports and significant imports, the US trade deficit had ballooned as well.

Some politicians took advantage of the disaffected population and ran successfully on an "America First" platform. While they were politically successful in the short term, closing borders and building walls, they did not bring about any positive change to the economy or the job market. Joblessness was still rampant, and it promoted associated issues like radicalization of the population. Inequality, poverty, substance abuse, crime and lawlessness shot up.

Interestingly, to make matters worse, automation was adopted in a big way by corporate America. Automation was ubiquitous in infrastructure, resources and other sectors including any remaining manufacturing in the US. This further accelerated Job losses while improving the bottom line of corporations. In the name of free market, companies lobbied for and amended laws in their favour. All profits continued to go to the top. Monopoly was facilitated and enabled. Inequality index went through the roof and there was no plan for the affected people.

Nader said, "I started my career in the creative

end of computing and that got offshored to India. Suddenly there weren't any interesting creative jobs around. US had lost the capacity to retain the cream; companies had started offshoring all work. I struggled for a while to find some work that was my passion and then I slowly started accepting any work that would come my way, just to put food on the table.

In the last twenty years, it has been one long slide, downhill. I know Emma doesn't think much of him, but Karan has been my support through all of this. He is pretty high in his merchant banking firm and is considered to be a brilliant and emerging star. You may say that he is driven, pushes hard and not really ethical in the business front, but on a personal front, he has done a lot for me. He would shell out and see me through my tough spots. Even my current role was his idea".

"What are you doing now?" asked Chen.

"I have started a business reclaiming occupied buildings in New York", said Nader.

"What do you mean?"

"Well, the jobless, the homeless, the poor, they don't have anywhere to stay. They have probably been evicted from their commission flats. They used to either live on the streets or under overpasses. But of late, with climate change, the winters have been more severe, and many people die on the streets.

And we have more and more trying to move to a safe shelter. Many have started occupying empty flats in residential buildings. They would just break in, plonk their stuff and stay put. The neighbours would leave the building, not wanting to live next to riffraff, and that empty flat will trigger more homeless to move in and so on. Before you know the building is occupied, the building owner doesn't see any revenue and the real estate value of the building has dropped. The building owner comes to me to clear the building".

"Are you saying that the situation has come to this in New York?"

"Oh yes. It has been going that way for a while now. The streets of New York are dangerous with rampant poverty and lawlessness. The very few moneyed people live in private gated communities well outside of New York. Unless you have the know-how and the backup, you would not walk the streets there. Probably one of the most dangerous places. Once I wanted Karan to come and see what we do. He just went nuts", said Nader.

***

As Nader entered Karan's suite, Karan gestured him to take a seat and pour himself a drink. Karan's collection was good, and Nader helped himself to a rare single malt.

Karan was on the phone and obviously Nader

couldn't hear the other side of the conversation.

Karan's voice was a tad high saying, "Look, money stays in the hands of a few. Wall Street is happy. Who gives a rat's arse about main street? Boohoo, they are in a sad shape", Karan listened and nodded for a while and said, "of course, it is the free market economy in full flow. You know the beauty of the market? It is pure, incorruptible. It is absolute democracy in action. No one dictator can foresee or change what is going to happen. No one person can swing it. Trust me, people have tried and have been burnt pretty bad. So here is my question. What makes you the friggin' genius to propose something different?"

There was more listening, and Nader could see Karan getting agitated and angry this end. Karan took off, "Ethical, moral obligations, my foot. To whom? For what? If you want to survive, come in and play the game or else stay out. Do not come in and ask for leniency. You will be killed. I will personally kill you if you are no good. I bust my ass to make sure this company makes money, and my shareholders are happy. In my business world, my stock price is my only friend, philosopher and guide.

Look, I do not want to waste my time anymore discussing this. I want the agreement signed and in my inbox in fifteen minutes, and that is it", Karan ended the phone conversation. He turned around to

Nader and said, "Sorry about that mate. He just had to be put in his place. How is the drink? I just got it delivered from the brewery near Glengyle".

Nader gave a thumbs-up and said, "Smoky heaven. By the way, the business has really taken off, thanks to you".

"Congratulations. Good to hear that. By the way how are you managing it?" asked Karan who had also loaned some money to Nader to start this business.

"I have put a team together. Lots of Russians and eastern Europeans, tough guys. I clear the building and get it back to the owner for a fee.

The first few operations went reasonably well. I was expecting a lot more action and had pumped up the amount of ammo my people carried. There were only a few lives lost. I lost one of my team members. Looks like most of the occupiers are just poor desperate people with nowhere to go", said Nader.

"Makes sense", said Karan, "getting armed means money and if they had had the money why would they hole up in such a place? By the way, how do you evict them and where to?"

"I just cut off the services, power, water, heat and such for a couple of days. Some of the occupants leave, but some stay on. You don't want to do this for too long as the occupants stink up the place with no water and it becomes a big clean-up job for my team later.

I then send in my team, well-armed, and prod the occupants out with their belongings. We use big duffel bags as it is easier to dump their stuff in one bag and escort them out to the street".

"And where do they go?" asked Karan.

"Well, down the road, probably to occupy another building and that becomes a perennial source of business for me", Nader smiled. "By the way, I make it clear to my client that they need to engage my services on a maintenance basis to keep their building free. We can clear it and clean it, but the homeless are going to come back unless we have a security detail to keep the building free of encroachment".

Karan was shaking his head when Nader said, "As I mentioned, we are celebrating our anniversary tomorrow at a building site in the Village. Just a small ceremony before the team goes in. I would like you to come".

Karan was taken aback and said, "Are you crazy. I am not getting down there. No one touches the surface today man. I haven't been there in ages and I wouldn't be caught in that hell hole that is the New York street.

Look, you are down there to run your business. But I would suggest that you increase your security detail and reduce your exposure. Your risk is not so much from inside the building; it will be more from the street where people know of you as the boss man with money. You are a prime target for a kidnapping".

***

As the group was near Phnom Kulen waterfalls, Nader sighed and said, "If only we had taken the people issue seriously and incorporated it in our FrICE solution".

"But we never really adopted the FrICE solution, did we? All we did was adopt the technology to automate everything, reduce the cost and build up corporate profits. We clearly highlighted this as an issue even during our school project", said Emma.

Nader agreed, "True, we let the extreme voices dominate. Those with vested interests and no vision wrote the American script. We are paying the price for it today. If only we had done it differently".

CODA

50 Years Later

The Driverless Truck

The bright and clean chrome bumper and kangaroo guard highlighted the brilliant blue hue of the truck cabin. Meg gave it a pat, turned around to Joe and said, "Well, that is the last one".

Joe grimaced. It was very obvious that Joe was going to miss the cabin. That was his last truck with a cabin and it was being retired.

With driverless trucks having been successfully introduced over two decades back, the new trucks rolling out did not have any driver cabins. The driving gear was at the wheel and the newer trucks looked more like a trailer with a fashionable control strip around it housing the sensors, cameras and the control hardware.

"You are one romantic truck driver", Meg laughed as they both moved from the truck to the adjacent café in the truck hub.

It had been a longish haul, Meg thought, as they

sat down for a cup of coffee. "We have come a long way, haven't we?" asked Joe, almost reading her mind. Meg smiled and nodded in agreement saying, "Morty was not way off, you know. When he nominated twenty years for a step change, we thought he was mad. Life certainly teaches you stuff".

Once FrICE was implemented, the first phase of change in Logistics was to minimize greenhouse gas emission. Australia adopted the ROLA strategy, the piggyback transportation approach. Container traffic adopted an intermodal approach with containers loaded on to trains and being retrieved at the destination hubs by trucks.

Australia converted their rail infrastructure to clean energy. Rail locomotives were powered by green hydrogen-based fuel, generated from clean renewable energy sources. They decided to convey road trucks and containers by rail, between major cities. The trains delivered the trucks and containers to hubs along the way and the trucks continued to cover the various interior towns and villages completing the logistics circuit.

This strategy delivered a substantial reduction in greenhouse gas emission while the trucking industry was gradually converting to clean fuel. This approach also delivered a significant reduction in labour requirement. Typically, the truck driver was required only from the hub to the warehouse, which was a very small portion of the total travel time between cities. The truck drivers stopped long-distance travel and were limited to loading and unloading the trucks on trains and collecting and delivering the cargo in the city or regional towns and villages.

With this change, the driver's quality of life improved with shorter and more reasonable shifts; there was improved health and well-being with elimination of long periods of sedentary activity, consistent and better-quality family time and better engagement with the local community.

In phase two, the last mile solution was implemented. Dedicated roadways from the railway depot hub to distribution warehouses were established. Fully automated driverless trucks delivered at the warehouse and were unloaded and loaded by robots. With the advent of green hydrogen-powered truck engines, this local truck movement also became people and greenhouse gas emission free.

As Meg and Joe finished their coffee, Meg could see her friends coming over. After the initial greetings and hugs, Meg said, "I think it is best if we move to the virtual experience centre". The group did. Nader, Chen, Emma and Miya had come back to Melbourne to celebrate the 50th anniversary of their FrICE presentation in school. Sam, Meg's daughter, was a project manager for some of the FrICE implementation projects and was providing the group with an update on how things unfolded in Australia.

In the virtual experience centre, while Sam was working on the set up, Meg was providing an overview on the energy and mining implementations.

Meg said, "The energy solution pretty much went to plan. The FrICE board had set out a marketing campaign on what was required of an NFP to be successful in FrICE energy tenders. The campaign inspired like-minded people, with a passion for energy transition, to come together, form NFPs and respond to the tenders. There was good level of response from various NFPs. More to the point, there was excellent response from the investing general public.

Solar took off in a big way. The government, through the FrICE board, allocated large swathes of land for commercial solar. Commercial solar became dominant under the debt-repayment model. Roof top solar also contributed in a big way.

Over a period of time, when the capital cost reduced, wind farms also took off. Currently solar and wind are the major contributors of clean renewable energy in Australia. Coal power is completely shut down and nuclear never took off here.

In terms of energy storage, once again things went

to plan. We have a combination of pumped hydro up in the snowy mountains, liquid air and flow battery storage facilities in the cities and clean hydrogen in salt caverns feeding our grid.

We are now sitting at around 200% of our original energy requirement. Obviously, this additional available energy is bringing in a lot of FrICE manufacturing businesses here to Australia. We are also selling some of the surplus energy to the rest of the world as clean renewable hydrogen in the form of ammonia and syngas".

"That is impressive", said Emma. "So how did the mining transition go?"

"We stuck to the NFP-based debt-repayment plan for mining. We provided the NFPs with free energy, didn't charge them any royalty for the ore or any import duties for their fully automated machinery. Mining output started becoming free over twenty years back. Since then, more and more mining operations have joined FrICE. Currently any ore requirement for FrICE is free. Local FrICE downstream operations take priority over international FrICE operations. Some of the ore is sold in the market as well. It is interesting to note that FrICE mining operations supported over 150,000 impacted people and their families through this transition", explained Meg.

"I got involved in the so-called mining transition

in South America and that was a disaster", responded Emma. "They did not start off with the free energy strategy. Instead, they jumped straight into mining and nationalized the mining operations. There was a court battle, and the government ended up compensating the shareholders for the drop in their share price. At the end, it was about the same cost as if they had purchased the mine in an open market. After this opening move, the FrICE strategy was abandoned for other political considerations.

No money was spent on automation of the mines and the people cost remained. Further, with every election, the government promised more jobs in the mine to get votes and the people cost kept spiraling up.

In the meantime, the government started its own steel mill with minimal automation. The labour cost issue was the same as in the mine. The mine was providing free ore to the steel mill, but their iron ore was not competitive in the international market. So, the government was forced to sell all the ore to the mill. The mill continued to make steel, but the steel price was not competitive as the people and energy cost were high.

With no real reduction in inputs like automation, labour or clean free energy, there was no outcome that was really free, but the government kept pushing it as free. They could only do this internally, and when they tried to sell it in the international market, they were priced out, too expensive". Emma concluded by saying, "The worst is that the politicians in North America now show this as an example of what FrICE does to the economy and justify their decision to oppose FrICE".

"That is a bit sad", said Chen. "In China, things were very different. The Chinese government adopted the FrICE concept and went on a spree of modernization. All mines were replaced with fully automated infrastructure over two decades. Mining workers were retrained and redeployed. In a couple of decades, with free energy and no people, the mine ore became cost free. And China has carried through with the FrICE approach, for the rest of the economy, at a breakneck speed".

"If not for Australia and a few other countries, China could have been the sole economic ruler of the world today", pointed out Miya.

Chen said, "It is interesting how the advent of abundant free clean energy has impacted the fossil fuel market. The global oil business has significantly declined. Oil platforms and refineries are closing down. Markets are able to buy these assets at throwaway prices today. In Asia, Malaysia has taken this option and has gotten into FrICE manufacturing of petroleum products, such as petrochemicals and plastics, in a big way. Interestingly, countries in the Middle East are trying to transition to an oil-free economy. They have invested in renewables and are pushing solar-based clean hydrogen in a big way for exports".

"Australia is FrICE trading with Malaysia", Meg said, "for the limited plastic that downstream will require to manufacture heavy industrial equipment".

Sam, who had just finished setting up the virtual experience system, added, "The FrICE transactions seem to be working well on block chain technology".

"In USA, the concept of free market economy is reigning supreme. Some oil majors have hedged their bets and are now promoting themselves as energy majors. They are actively engaged in the renewable energy sector. Others, with major investment in oil infrastructure, want to protect their investment and are actively working with the government to limit renewables or at least get their investment back", added Nader.

Nader paused, smiled and said, "Free market rules, till it doesn't go your way and then the government needs to bail you out.

And in the spirit of free market, nothing is for free. The erstwhile commercial model still rules, inequality rules and we are seeing a massive shift from immigration to emigration. The brain drain is just mind boggling".

CHAPTER 2

Virtual Visits

Sam gently cleared her throat and let the group know that the virtual experience system was ready to go. The group followed her to the virtual experience pod. Before entering the pod, Sam said, "The Australian approach to automation was down to the first principle – people safety. We decided to segregate people from automated machines – be it robots in factories or truck movements in highways.

It made good sense. This approach certainly made it safer for people, for sure. But what it also did was enable machines and factories to be automated much earlier, with less sophisticated software and AI.

With this segregation approach, it was also easier to approve and implement new AI-based systems immediately. The effectiveness of the AI only had impact on the productivity, not on people safety; the worst-case scenario was damage to machines, not to people.

Due to this approach, Australia was able to have completely automated factories much earlier, compared to certain other countries. However, physical visits to most of these businesses, mines and factories are banned, for the same reason. People physically enter these facilities only when necessary and called upon. Of course, anyone can virtually visit every part of the facility".

Sam paused, looked around and said, "let's jump in".

As they immersed into the virtual world, the aerial view showed huge swathes of solar installations visible at a distance. The complex sprawled over hundreds of kilometres long and wide. Sam said, "This industrial complex is predominantly focused on producing machines for the energy and mining sector. At one end, you can view the steel mills and other metal processing factories. In the next sector are the component manufacturers".

Sam took them through the steel mill that was over twenty years old. "This is one of the first factories to be built in this industrial complex. We term this a first-generation automated factory. The AI is fairly basic. The factory is mostly people free; most of the people tasks have been automated and is being done by machines. Some people, located offsite, still operate and control the plant. The maintenance still requires physical presence of people. Sections of this factory will be completely shut down prior to maintenance people coming on site".

As they zoomed out of the factory, Sam explained that in the intervening twenty years, AI had improved by leaps and bounds. As they virtually threaded their way through the next factory, Sam said, "This is what we called the third-generation AI plant where the automation is elegant, efficient and effective. All plant activities here are carried out by machines with no people interaction". The visitors could see some parts of the plant were not operating and the machines were being taken apart by terrestrial robots and drones. Sam pointed out saying, "automated, people-free maintenance. The robots and drones are located in the regional hubs. They come over and conduct the requisite maintenance in all third-generation factories in this zone".

They started moving again and Sam took the team across to other Shuru factories – factories that use the steel and other metals and raw materials to make machines and components for mining and other manufacturing activities. She pointed out to the solar panel manufacturing factory and other factories that made mining haul trucks.

Sam said, "The haul truck manufacturers get the tyres from Malaysia through FrICE Contracts.

We have similar contracts with FrICE manufacturers from India for machines like motors, gearboxes and pumps, typically used in all sectors".

"Is this cash-free trade?" asked Nader.

"Well, since FrICE has moved away from monetary value, the energy-based e'value is used for FrICE trading between economies. The new accounting system assigns a nominal e'value to a product or material based on the median energy that went into making it", said Meg.

Chen turned to Miya and said, "Remember our trip to the sugarcane plantation and the Sugar Mill?" Miya nodded with a smile and turned around to Sam, "Hey Sam, can we take a look at those?"

"Sure", said Sam. The group was now hovering over a sugarcane plantation. Sam was pointing to people free, fully automated farm machinery. "The machines are all running on hydrogen-based fuel. They are located in regional hubs and service all cane farms in the region", said Sam.

As they zoomed through the cane, Sam pointed out to small boxes bedded in the soil saying, "These are permanently installed soil condition monitors. They check the soil for salinity, assess the water table and direct water flows accordingly. With any anticipated water deficit, our desalination plants will kick in and fill up the reservoirs, in advance.

Drones do random soil sampling and testing for nutrients, as required. Fertilizer is delivered and stored in sheds by automated delivery trucks. Automated fertilizer delivery system mixes fertilizer and drip-irrigates the crop".

As they came out of the sugarcane plantation, Sam pointed out to drones taking crop samples to check for infestation. "Any crop dusting is done by specialized drones".

From the farm, Sam took the team through a completely automated factory making sugar from cane. Machines were humming, cane was being crushed and the fugals were extracting sugar from the liquor. There was not a person in site.

On the way out, Sam said, "Let me take you to a fruit plantation". In there, they could see drones checking and monitoring the condition of fruit. "These drones are pretty handy", Sam said. "They locate and assign 3D GPS coordinates for each fruit. They check the fruit for infestations and report on the same. They are also used for crop dusting as required".

"Yeah. If you can recognize faces why not check on fruit condition", said Emma. "By the way, don't they pick the fruit?"

"In some farms, they do. But this seems to be a better solution", said Sam pointing to little caterpillar-like robots perched on the branches.

"These caterpickers are rechargeable robots that have pincers to cut the fruit stem. They can climb the tree and proceed to their assigned fruit based on the 3D GPS from the drones. On reaching the fruit, they get on it and cut the stem. The fruit drops and is caught by the conical net at the bottom of the tree. The fruit rolls down the net and is collected at the bottom of the tree. The fruit is then moved to the collection shed through automated conveyors.

And when they are low on charge, they just go down to the docking station at the foot of the tree and get charged. What is interesting is that these caterpickers are on a neural network; there is no command and comply. They talk to each other, agree on which caterpicker does what and seem to do a pretty good job".

"Cool", responded Emma.

"Let us take a look at a dairy farm", said Chen.

"There are not that many dairy farms nowadays", said Sam. "Over the last twenty years, it is predominantly manufactured meat and milk, made in factories. The cost of manufactured meat and milk dropped to zero, with FrICE, and that just shook up the natural meat and dairy industries. The ethical aspect of not wanting to kill an animal was the trigger that finished them off.

The manufactured meat and milk has been a

big hit with our generation and onwards. We get a quality product, well controlled, with no unwanted pathogens and you will not be able to taste or smell any difference. Today, I seriously couldn't touch meat that was from a real animal", Sam shuddered.

"However, we have some old people who still insist on the natural meat and dairy, and we have a few farms operating to satisfy their needs. Let us go to one of those", said Sam.

The farm was picturesque with green grass and a flowing brook gurgling through.

The cows were gently ambling towards the milking sheds. Sam indicated that the feed had changed. "Their feed nowadays has an infused additive, a kind of seaweed, that significantly reduces the methane emissions to the point where they are not classified as contributing to climate change anymore".

The group could see drones herding the cows into the stall. As the cows entered the milking stalls, Sam pointed to the permanent sensor station mounted that identified each and every cow through facial recognition and measured the animal's basic parameters like height, weight and blood pressure. Infrared cameras got a temperature map of the animal while retinal scans were conducted, and a primary analysis was conducted on the cow's breath sample. The readings and results were displayed in the screen.

"If any of these basic parameters indicate abnormality, the cow is quarantined automatically, and drones collect further samples of blood, urine and dung and send it away for more detailed tests. The cow is either taken off the facility and transported to a vet clinic or is sent back to the herd depending on the test results".

Sam smiled and said, "These cows are probably getting better health care than you people did, fifty years back".

The group watched the milking system automatically latching on and milking the cow. Sam said, "The milk is automatically pumped to chilled holding tanks and once processed is either pumped into pipes that take it to the adjacent milk factory or pumped to the driverless milk trucks that take it to factories elsewhere".

And there was not a person to be seen anywhere in the farm.

Sam turned to the group and said, "Let me take you guys to a recycling facility before we wrap up. I think you will like it. One good thing about a virtual tour to recycling is the lack of smell".

As they zoomed in to the recycling facility, the place looked more like a factory.

"All manufactured items have embedded identity

either coded or chipped. Sorting starts at individual households where the smart bins will alarm and minimize cross contamination. Here sensors and sorters further segregate waste based on its embedded identity and processes it in dedicated recycling lines that address material like copper, steel or LDPE, a particular type of plastic", said Sam.

Moving on to the industrial waste section, they could see robots dismantling machines coming in at the end of their life. The dismantled components, in turn, were being sorted and binned based on the constituent material. At the end of the facility was the crushing plant that converted the segregated waste to billets.

As the group stepped off the virtual experience pod, they thanked Sam for her time. "So, we understand that you were involved in some of these FrICE projects. Are you still doing the same?" asked Emma.

"Well, not really", said Sam, "I have an active interest in food technology and have been dabbling in that space for the last few years. Interestingly, my latest product is an ice cream".

The group groaned "oh no" in unison. Sam burst out laughing.

CHAPTER 3

Free Ice Cream

"But seriously, there is still a market for new stuff and more to the point, people are creating new things. That is great", said Miya.

"Well, I had an idea for an aerated explosive ice cream bar", said Sam, "and I made some samples. When I tried it out, the explosion of flavours and taste in my mouth was just amazing. It was clear that this ice cream had real potential.

So, I discussed the concept with a friend of mine, who is also a food technologist, about making this a commercial venture. She tasted the ice cream and was sold on the idea. We brought in a business designer and a marketing expert and formed a team.

We did some market research and the results were positive. Our marketing partner then embarked on a marketing strategy, identifying platforms and portals to reach end users and developing impactful media that would penetrate the market segment effectively.

The other food technologist took the product through the FDA approval process.

I took the product design role. I registered our recipe and our intent to manufacture this ice cream with the FrICE manufacturing register. Through the registry, we confirmed cost free availability of all ingredients required by the recipe.

I also registered the recipe and the manufacturing methodology at the patents register. We would retain rights to the recipe for ten years, from when we start commercial manufacturing. After that, the recipe goes into public domain; anyone can use this recipe from then on.

Our business partner explored availability and capacity of ice cream manufacturing pods in the local area. He confirmed that they have the necessary equipment to execute the process on the recipe and produce this ice cream. He located five pods spread over a few suburbs and booked them".

"Could you just walk in and get these machines to produce whatever you want?" asked Emma.

"Not really. There is a queue system. Start-ups and new innovations tend to get pod slots to kick off their product. But it follows supply and demand. If there is a huge demand for our ice cream in that suburb, FrICE will automatically add manufacturing pod capacity in that suburb", responded Sam.

Sam continued, "As a group, we agreed on a three-phased strategy to establish the ice cream in the market. In the first phase, the ice cream will be offered for free to entice people to try it out. In phase two, the ice cream will be offered at a price. Depending on the response in phase one, we would mark a suitable price for the ice cream in phase two".

"So, it is not free ice cream after all", said Emma.

"The shopping strip has at least five ice cream machines that give free ice cream. It is just that we think our ice cream is amazing and special. So, we are going to charge for it. End of the day, the people decide. If people think it is good enough to pay for, they will. Let us keep in mind, people do not have money sloshing around anymore. It is fairly scarce".

"And if your ice cream does not sell enough, what happens?" asked Emma.

"We will drop the price first. If that doesn't do the trick, we will drop the price model and will instead offer the ice cream for a set number of SMEPs, social media engagement points", said Sam.

"They have taken off in a big way in the last couple of decades", agreed Nader.

"Yes, SMEPs have emerged as a powerful mode of value exchange, an alternate to currency. SMEPs are excellent marketing tools. We can use them to push the product far and wide. Further likes, forwards, rewards and other similar acknowledgements have the effect of raising my profile in the wider society", said Meg.

"You know, an enhanced profile could get people an influencer status gaining them preferential entry to clubs, seats at concerts and so on. An innovator is considered an active social contributor, and this incentivizes many to get into this space", said Miya.

Sam turned to Emma and said, "And if the ice cream still does not sell, then we will have to offer it for free".

"Why do that. Why not close shop. I mean take your product off the list and walk away, if no one wants to even give you a SMEP?" asked Emma.

"Well, in a world where there is no price on things and people could go and get the best, the fact that some of them come for your product means your product is the best, for those people. That is still no small achievement", said Meg.

"True", said Sam, "Most of the ice creams that you get for free are really amazing and are branded. They are for free, either because the IP ran out or because they were priced out. If you look up the creator online, you would typically find the demand numbers for their products highlighted in their profile, with a sense of pride.

Now, let's all go to the local shopping centre. You

guys can try out my ice cream".

As they reached the local shopping strip, Sam said, "We are not a very innovative bunch. We took the earlier model of local strip shops, suburban Shopping Centres and regional malls and replicated the same under FrICE. Instead of shops, we now have manufacturing pods, dispensing machines and product outlets. The malls also act as a place for people to congregate, for concerts and local cultural events".

The group tasted Sam's ice cream. Everyone agreed it tasted amazing.

Sam pointed out to the other ice creams on the display menu and said, "Free ice cream, all of it". Sam paused and continued, "You guys visited an actual factory that you could walk through when you did your school project. This is just a small manufacturing pod, looks more like a vending machine. It mixes all the ingredients and gives me the ice cream that I want, for free. And if it can't, it will let me know where I can get it from or will get the other machine to deliver it to where I want.

And to think the whole world had to go through all these FrICE hoops to get here! Isn't that just ridiculous?" she shook her head with a cheeky smile.

Meg, Emma, Chen and Miya gave Sam a real dark look.

THE END